Assessing Information Needs: tools, techniques and concepts for the Internet age

Second edition

INFORMATION MANAGEMENT

Published by Aslib, The Association for Information Management and Information Management International
Staple Hall
Stone House Court
London EC3A 7PB
Tel: +44 020 7903 0000
Fax: +44 020 7903 0011
Email: *aslib@aslib.com*
WWW: *http://www.aslib.com*

ISBN 0 85142 432 5

Please note the ISBN
number shown above
is incorrect
The correct ISBN is
0851424333

Assessing Information Needs: tools, techniques and concepts for the Internet age

Second edition

David Nicholas

INFORMATION MANAGEMENT

Is your organisation a corporate member of Aslib?

Aslib, The Association for Information Management, is a world class corporate membership organisation with over 2000 members in some 70 countries. Aslib actively promotes best practice in the management of information resources. It lobbies on all aspects of the management of, and legislation concerning, information at local, national and international levels.

Aslib provides consultancy and information services, professional development training, conferences, specialist recruitment, Internet products, and publishes primary and secondary journals, conference proceedings, directories and monographs.

Further information is available from:

Aslib, The Association for Information Management
Staple Hall
Stone House Court
London EC3A 7PB
Tel: +44 020 7903 0000
Fax: +44 020 7903 0011
Email: *aslib@aslib.com*
WWW: *http://www.aslib.com/*

Series Editor

Sylvia Webb is a well-known consultant, author and lecturer in the information management field. Her first book, *Creating an Information Service*, now in its third edition, was published by Aslib and has sold in over forty countries. She has experience of working in both the public and private sectors, ranging from public libraries to national and international organisations. She has also been a lecturer at Ashridge Management College, specialising in management and interpersonal skills, which led to her second book, *Personal Development in Information Work*, also published by Aslib. She has served on a number of government advisory bodies and is past Chair of the Information and Library Services Lead Body which develops National Vocational Qualifications (NVQs) for the LIS profession. She is actively involved in professional education with Aslib and the Library Association and is also a former Vice-President of the Institute of Information Scientists. As well as being editor of this series, Sylvia Webb has written three of the Know How Guides: *Making a charge for library and information services*, *Preparing a guide to your library and information service* and *Knowledge management: linchpin of change*.

A complete listing of all titles in the series can be found at the back of this volume.

About the author

David Nicholas is Head of the Department of Information Science, City University. He is also Director of the Internet Studies Research Group. Current interests lie in the impact of the Internet on key strategic groups and the potential of web log analysis. Other interests include information and the media; information needs analysis and bibliometrics.

Contents

Acknowledgements

Many thanks to a number of people who have shaped and influenced my thinking. First of all to Maurice Line, whose early writings on the topic provide this guide with much of its structure. With the help of colleagues Chris Needham and Adrian Mole, at what was then known as the School Of Librarianship, Polytechnic of North London, these ideas were expanded and taken further. Many more people provided the data to clothe these ideas. In particular I would like to mention the names of: Peter Cole, Professor of Journalism, University of Sheffield; Helen Martin and David Hencke from *The Guardian*; Pete Williams and Paul Huntington, City University; and Tom Dobrowolski, University of Warsaw whose ideas have very much set the tone for the second edition.

Note to Second Edition

The second edition of this work examines more fully the role of the Internet in information needs assessments (hence the expanded sub-title). The Internet has become the ultimate Pandora's box. It is widely thought to be an information and communication cure-all – the information elixir of life, maybe. If that is the case then, perhaps, the meeting of information need will no longer prove to be the problem it has been in the past. The Guide considers this possibility and examines the way the Internet has changed the concept of what constitutes use and the user. A new term is introduced – the I-player, to describe the digital information user. The latest information platform, the mobile phone, is also examined in the context of information need.

The new edition provides more practical guidance regarding the conduct of information needs assessments – especially in interview form, and provides new examples taken from the author's most recent research projects[1,2] to illustrate the points being raised. Two more methods have been added to the range of methods discussed – web log analysis and focus groups.

As a result of all these changes and additions the Guide has grown in size and is now about 50% larger than its predecessor.

Notes

1. The Changing Information Environment: the impact of the Internet on Information seeking in the Media. British Library, 1997-1998

2. The global information consumer: web log analysis. Case studies: News International and *The Independent*, 1999-2000

1. Introduction

This Guide offers up a systematic method of identifying, evaluating and comparing information needs. Its purpose is to provide high quality, structured and standardised data that can be routinely fed into the design, evaluation and auditing of information systems, like the Internet, libraries, OPACs, and commercial on-line services. The thinking behind the Guide is that in the Information Wild West, in which we find ourselves, there is a great risk of information systems running wild – and running free of the (end) user. There is a real danger – and the danger signs are already there, that criticising information systems – the Internet is a case in point, is seen as being politically and educationally incorrect. The guide provides the wherewithal to put (beguilingly simple, but increasingly complex) information systems in their place – within an evaluatory framework, behind the user and not in front of them. Ironically, the author believes that it will be an information system – the Internet, that will, in fact, force information needs concerns to the top of the information agenda in the new millennium. The current concern with information passports to aid journeys into cyberspace offers some grounds for optimism. After all, without personalised information needs assessments, these passports will fail to get off the ground. Without these passports, or something similar, we are surely in for an information future of true Orwellian proportions.

The Guide, while expounding sound principles and an evaluatory framework, is not a theoretical document – there are far too many of these. What is proposed is based firmly on the findings of research projects involving hundreds of people and their use of information systems – usually as part of British Library funded projects, over a period of more than twenty years. The people studied have included scientists, journalists, politicians, social workers, stockbrokers, academics and the general public; and the systems studied have included libraries, OPACs, CD-ROMs, commercial online services and the Internet. It is from these studies of multifarious user groups and systems – and from interviewing numerous information needs 'guinea pigs' in classroom situations, that this Guide and its framework have obtained their literary warrant.

There are six sections to the Guide. The first section explains why information needs assessments are so important for information professionals, information consumers, information units and systems. The second section defines and maps out the terrain, delineating the whole information process. The various stages of the information seeking and finding process – from need to use or consumption – are ordered and described. The key terms that are associated with the study of information consumption are defined and discussed – not to be pedantic but to make it crystal clear what is being studied. Section three – in many ways the core section, lays out the essential characteristics of need. In all, eleven characteristics are identified and described: subject, function, nature, intellectual level, viewpoint, quantity, quality/authority, date range/

currency, speed of delivery, place of publication/ origin and processing and packaging. Section four examines the obstacles that people encounter when trying to meet their information needs and the constraints placed upon their information-seeking. Section five is somewhat different in nature from the earlier chapters. It provides a review of the available data collection methods for those wishing to conduct needs/user studies themselves or understand the significance of a particular user need survey. The Guide ends with a consideration of the information future.

2. Why Undertake Information Needs Assessments?

The main reason for undertaking needs assessments must be that the information profession has neglected doing so in the past and that has not got the information profession very far, and, indeed, continues to frustrate its progress. The profession lags behind most others in terms of salary, conditions, status and customer satisfaction, and many of its flagships, like public libraries, are heading towards the reefs – blown there by the hurricane force winds that have been generated by the Internet. While space-age information systems, such as the Internet, grace our information centres and libraries, we still do not use suitably modern and effective management methods to ensure that these systems are providing consumers with what they need and want. To say that information systems are largely free from consumer evaluation and are rarely challenged with user needs (or use) data, would be to exaggerate, but not to exaggerate by very much. Rarely are high quality data fed into the design, evaluation and running of information systems, like the Intranets, libraries, OPACs, and on-line services. But why should this be, for would anyone really doubt that libraries, librarians, information units and databases are there solely to service the needs of their clients?

There are six factors that we can attribute to the neglect of the user:

(1)   believe it or not, there are still many (quite eminent) information professionals who feel that it is not necessary to consult the client in, what they consider to be, professional matters;

(2)   information professionals tend to be preoccupied with information systems and not the users of these systems;

(3)   the profession is plagued by insular attitudes and poor communication skills, something that does not lead to close relationships with the consumer;

(4)   the expenditure of resources involved in the obtaining of needs data is not thought to be justified in these hard budgetary times;

(5)   an absence of a standard, commonly understood framework for the assessment of information needs – something, which it has to be said, lets information professionals off the hook;

(6)   it is by no means easy getting hold of the necessary needs data.

There is little point in conducting information needs assessments (trust us)

It is hard to credit, but there is a school of thought that believes there is very little point in consulting the users: they do not know what they are talking about, why ask them, far better to forget the topic and just trust professional judgement. Just listen to this: *there is something rather absurd in being constantly enjoined to meet the needs of the user, when needs have been probed the outcomes have been worse rather than better* (Shinebourne; 1980). Essentially, the argument is that we have got it right in the first place, it is just a question of convincing the users of it. Shinebourne has an unlikely ally in Cronin (1981), for despite claiming that *user studies are on the whole a jolly good idea,* he too has his reservations as to their practical worth: *a fine sentiment no doubt but sentiment is not always at home in the world of commerce.* What do information professionals know about commerce, you have every right to ask? Indeed, commerce is busy getting closer to the user. While people no longer say these kinds of things in print any more (they are politically incorrect), the attitudes they reflect are still endemic in the profession today. In fact, there has been a subtle shift in professional utterances, which reflects these politically correct and fast-changing times. It is now said that information needs assessments are an impossibility, because people do not know what their needs are and they cannot anticipate what they will be. No matter how packaged, these attitudes are a corrupting influence on the new generation of information professionals.

A systems-driven profession

The information profession is, by and large systems driven; it shows an enormous interest in the processing and storing of information, to the general neglect of the user. In the profession there is a marked fixation with powerful, innovative information systems, sometimes irrespective of their direct suitability to users. Once such systems are obtained it is on to the next powerful, innovative system, without any user evaluation of the former system. The sheer pace of technological change provides the ideal opportunity and excuse. The qualities that are appreciated are systems' characteristics, such as speed of response, storage size, number of network stations etc. In their deliberations and writings the systems-driven of this world pay due allegiance to the idea of the user (generally mentioning the dreaded phrase *user-friendly*, which is, of course, a wholly systems' phrase). If needs are considered at all they are generally done so purely in terms of how the system might meet these needs, rather than developed or changed to meet them. Information systems are omnipotent; users are too often the supplicants.

Two examples to drive the above point home. At a Multi-media conference the author attended a few years ago the 100 or so delegates, from the top media companies in the land, were asked how many of them had online access, CD-ROMs etc. With some alacrity all put up there hands. Yet, when asked how many of them conducted annual user needs assessments, just one did so. When confronted by the sheer disparity most felt uncomfortable at first but soon gathered their wits and asserted that this did not mean that they did not 'know' their clients. The main methodology for obtaining user data appeared to be osmosis. The second example. At an even more recent conference – this time Government librarians worried about their image, it transpired that not one of the

80 or so delegates had a policy towards end-users. Despite their massive and increasing presence in their organisations. If you don't have a policy for something as big as end use – and you work in a Government Department, then what do you have policies for you might rightly ask.

Poor communication skills, and insular and antagonistic attitudes

Information professionals too often demonstrate a marked reluctance to question their clients – often citing their shortage of time in their defence. But often the real reason is that information professionals – though they would inevitably protest otherwise – do not always know their clients as they patently should. A continuing dialogue between client and information professional is too often a rarity. This is partly to do with a characteristic insularity and four-wall mentality – they are insufficiently concerned with information problems that occur in the organisation outside the information unit– in the office or home for instance, and, as a result, information professionals seldom see, or interact with, the client in the workplace. It is in the office and home that information needs are hatched – and only occasionally, one would have thought, in the information unit.

Poor lines of communication can also be attributed to the low status of information professionals in the organisation, making it difficult for them to initiate contact – they are generally supplicants in the information exchange. Also, it is not an exaggeration to say that a good number of information workers are antagonistic towards their users – such antagonism is bred of long and close proximity with them. It is an old cliché, but for battle-weary information professionals people get in the way of the systems they are so busily building/defending. Communication skills courses at Library/Information schools are beginning to tackle the problem, but it is quite plain to all those that teach these courses that students find it more difficult to master oral skills than written skills.

Expensive to collect the data

Another reason for neglecting information needs is that the data does not come cheap and the financial trade-off is not immediately obvious. Typically, you have to survey large numbers of busy – and sometimes difficult – people on a regular basis. This it is argued would cost – take money away from the Book Fund (the information professionals' original ultimate threat) or Intranet developments (the new ultimate threat); remove staff from critical front-line library routines, like shelving books or updating the Web site. With these comforting thoughts information professionals give up the ghost of the information needs survey. But, what is the point of efficiently overseeing a collection or site that bears only a dim and distant reflection of the needs of its users? And, in a world that has probably seen more change in the workplace in the last five years than in the previous fifty, how can we be so sure that the information unit reflects all these changes, and that is heading along the right track? The correct and only view must surely be that it is too costly *not* to collect needs data. The stance must surely be that, in these dynamic and fast-changing times, it is wholly *economic* to collect this data on a regular and on-going basis. But it is not going to be easy to convince people of the wisdom of this. At a recent short course, when the author explained that needs data was best collected by interview and that the interview might take 45 minutes a number of participants audibly choked – the implication was obvious, that is a lot of time. But 45 minutes to ensure that someone gets the service they need and deserve? Would anybody choke if they were told it would take 10 hours to design a web site that few people would use? I doubt it.

Lack of a commonly understood and agreed framework of analysis

There are few easily understood and practical frameworks available with which to explore people's needs. Existing discussions have tended to be too theoretical and academic. Rather than clarify the situation, more often than not they have muddied the waters; rather than encouraging people to conduct user needs surveys, in fact they have provided them with an excuse not to do so. What is really needed is an analytical, off-the-shelf model that can operate in the hurly-burly of today's high-tech information centres and units. Maurice Line (1969; 1974) offered up a suitable model many years ago, but it has not been widely adopted. This guide embraces and expands upon Line's original model.

The main intention is to provide a practical, usable and reusable method of analysing information needs that can be employed by information managers, information system designers and information workers alike.

No single or easy method of collecting the data

Of course, the method of analysis is only going to be as good as the data that is fed into it. For everything to work the data collection methods have to be effective and robust. When it comes to data collection methods there is a rich choice of methods. In fact, the problem is really one of too much choice, and that, too, puts people off. The best ones are typically the most expensive to use (interview and observation) and the ones that offer the most data, most cheaply (web log analysis, citations and issue statistics) provide a (blurred) insight into use rather than need.

There are good and pressing reasons why the neglect of the information needs cannot continue. The reasons are these:

(1)   the huge and rising costs of computerisation will demand that systems be evaluated in the light of overall need, not just the need of the information professional, but with reference to everybody in the organisation;

(2)   the increased rigour with which information units are being audited and questioned over how they spend money will require that information

services collect data on their clients to justify themselves;

(3)   increased competition from Web-based services and competitive tendering from within and without the profession will force information services to get closer to their customers (or go to the wall);

(4)   the huge growth in end-use will so unnerve information professionals, worried about their jobs, that they will be forced to monitor closely what their customers are thinking, doing and wanting;

(5)   the Internet – and the Information Society it ushers in, will require information need data if they are to move to the next stage of their development.

Cost of computerisation

With vast sums of money being spent on computerised communication and retrieval systems (e.g. Intranets, Web sites), mistaken judgements have increasingly serious and perilous consequences. With the rapidity of change goes increased risk. It is only through an understanding of what information people need and how they set about finding it that information professionals can ensure that suitable information systems are provided – professional judgement alone cannot be relied upon, and certainly not in these fast-changing times. There is a complicating factor at work though, for today many of the computerised information systems that we work with are designed by people outside the profession – typically from the computing field; and because the value of the 'library' market is just a drop in the ocean for computer companies, systems are not necessarily designed specifically with the needs of 'our' customers in mind. Therefore mistakes can easily be made. Expensive information systems rarely used or frequently replaced do not look good on the audit sheet and do a lot in terms of alienating the customer.

Accountability and auditing

Information needs data are an essential part of value-for-money exercises. Recent political and economic events have dragged libraries and information centres into the value-driven environment, from which they are unlikely ever to escape. They are now on the same cost-conscious footing as any other business and, as a result, they are subject to the same concerns such as customer care, customer charters, cost benefit and the like. Whilst this is generally recognised as a *fait accompli* by the profession, few seem to realise that these concerns are nothing but a sham unless they are underpinned by the systematic collection of data on customer needs, their perceptions of service delivery etc. How else is performance to be measured? Certainly not anymore by the traditional measure of the number of books and serials on the shelves or new titles bought per year. However, the number and power of the computers on display have superseded this measure in recent times. The yardstick has to be changed for it is only through customer satisfaction that success or effectiveness can be truly measured – and satisfaction can only be obtained by meeting user need. It is customers that we should be proudly showing off – not machines or shelves. To place the customer care charter on show in the main library, scatter a few complaints forms around and employ a number of staff to monitor a service that in most cases is woefully inadequate, is too often the common response.

Competition and deregulation

Because of the opening out of the information market as a result of a combination of political, economic and technological factors (especially the Internet), if information professionals do not get close to the user others will. Whatever the reasons for the profession's neglect of information needs, it is surely because of it, that, in this so-called information society, information centres and information professionals are frequently under attack, in danger of losing their jobs, having their salaries depressed, increasingly marginalised and losing market share etc. And this must be more true of public libraries than of any other organisation. Also, who would bet against Web-delivered digital libraries succeeding over cold, remote, academic or government libraries in the market for customers?

The profession should look to successful businesses for guidance on how to survive the new economic climate. The advice of the Chairman of Kingfisher, the Woolworth, B&Q and Superdrug group, is certainly worth taking on board: *we are concerned with meeting end-consumer needs. If you look at the success or failure of many organisations, the root of the problem often comes back to not anticipating how custom-*

er's needs have changed, and therefore not adapting to those changes. (Kay, 1994). Sound advice, indeed.

The end-user cometh and cometh again and again

Related to the above point about changes in the marketplace, there is also the rapidly expanding armoury of computers, modems, online services, CD-ROMs etc. that are being built up in people's homes and offices. During the Eighties the profession constantly debated the outcome of end-use – some doubting whether it would ever happen and others forecasting the Apocalypse. Since then the likes of Textline, NEXIS and FT Profile have been joined by even more user-friendly CD-ROMs; and most recently we have been visited by the ultimate in user friendliness – the Internet. The number of end-users has risen from no more than a few dozen in the early 1970s to millions today. Nobody is questioning these figures, the permanence or fickleness of end-use anymore, but few seem to be researching the consequences. The reaction of too many people in the profession is rather like that of a frightened rabbit in a car's headlights. They are paralysed by fear. The correct reaction is surely to recognise that there is now much common ground, a common vocabulary, a willingness to discuss information problems; and the opportunity should be grabbed with both hands. The potential terrain for the information professional has increased enormously, although most of it lies outside the physical boundaries of the information unit. The key to conquering this terrain, of course, is information needs assessments. When you talk about end-users you are really talking about information needs.

The Internet (and the Information Society)

The Information Society will never become a reality until we can genuinely meet people's individual and special needs; just broadcasting ever-greater amounts of information is not what it is about. We talk glibly about the commodification of information but essentially we – and the systems we provide, are crude batch processors. Information products are incredibly raw and general – even in the case of the Web, search success depends largely on the lucky dip of single keywords or the input of a hieroglyphic (URLs). There is a mistaken belief amongst the profession that the future is all about sharing information – knowledge management style, or storing and distributing information – digital library style, but it is, in fact, about getting closer to what people need in the way of information and producing it in a processed, packaged form for the individual to consume at a particular point in time that they choose. Customisation, individualisation, segmentation in the information market – the next stage of the information revolution – can only come on the back of personal detail and knowledge. The future of information provision is surely personalised information flows – it would be an extremely brave (foolish?) person who would argue against that. And how else do you get personal information other than from information needs assessments?

The World Wide Web, with its enormous information reach, its ability to provide undreamed-of quantities of information with just a couple of clicks of the mouse, and the way it has made information science a concern of the general public, has surely demonstrated the value – and set the scene, for information needs analysis. Surely, also, it has demonstrated the limitations of information use measures (hits, visits etc) when used on their own – something we shall return to later. The Web's influence is a complex one. It offers the prospect of meeting – and unearthing, all kinds of information needs. Needs can be met with less effort. It also provides an enormous stimulus and is capable of uncovering all kinds of dormant information needs. The Web meets information needs, triggers information needs and attracts people –information voyeurs, who have no needs at all. It has turned information-seeking into a global past time. And it also routinely maps – through Web logs – the information trails that are made as people attempt to meet those needs.

For many people the Internet has resulted in the overnight transformation of an information-poor world into an information-rich world. We have moved from a world in which information needs were rarely ever effectively met – certainly not without a tremendous expenditure of effort and cost, to one in which they are 'potentially' only too easily met. This has created something in the way of a culture shock – to both information intermediary and end-user. What is ironic, is that in the information rich environment in which we find ourselves, we need to be even more clear about our information needs than ever before. What else is going to provide us with the precision for our searches, the filters for the push technology; what else is going to help us steer a path through the information jungle (certainly not any of the current Web search engines)? It would not be difficult to envisage, that in five years time we will all carry information passports; these passports would essentially be our information needs profiles, which we could take from system-to-system, file-to-file.

3. What Are Information Needs?

People talk about information need without ever bothering to define it. Sometimes there are very good reasons for not doing so, for when definitions are provided, they are often vague or highly complex in nature – clouding further some already muddy water, and really serve very little practical use. Despite years of academic debate and much intellectual borrowing from other disciplines, like management and psychology, not a lot has emerged that would aid the practitioner in their day-to-day information needs deliberations.

People often talk about information needs when, in fact, they are referring to wants or use. While both are plainly manifestations of need – and should be considered, they are different and do not fully or accurately describe need. We should be evaluating the need people have for information, the wants they express for it, and the demands and use they make of it. Despite the difficulties and complexities involved in needs analysis, the solution is not to rely wholly on use indicators, such as web site 'hits'. In football parlance, route one football – simply kicking the ball forward as far as you can, is not the answer.

Therefore, as part and parcel of any definition, you need to set about distinguishing information needs from some closely associated, but distinct, information concepts, like use, which are frequently (sometimes deliberately) confused with information needs – to the general detriment of information system design and provision. This section follows much of Maurice Line's thinking, as set out in his article *Draft definitions: information and library needs, wants, demands and uses* (1974).

Information needs: a working definition

For Line (1969) information needs were seen as the *information* [that] *would further this job or this research, and would be recognised as doing so by the recipient*. Information needs arise when a person recognises a gap in his/her state of knowledge and wishes to resolve that anomaly – *an anomalous state of knowledge*, as another commentator put it (Belkin, 1989). One can build upon these definitions by adding that it is the information that individuals *ought* to have to do their job effectively, solve a problem satisfactorily or pursue a hobby or interest happily. The operative word is surely 'ought'. There is an implied value judgement here – the meeting of need is beneficial or necessary to the person – and would be recognised as such. We all make assumptions that for people to perform efficiently, effectively, safely, happily etc. they need to be well informed. i.e. that their information needs should be met.

Of course, most people do not have information needs *per se*, rather they experience a problem or difficulty or are under some pressure, and these cognitive and emotional needs may be met, or partially met, by obtaining and then applying that information. Information needs arise out of a desire to meet one or other of the three basic human needs: physiological needs (need for food, shelter etc.); psychological needs (need for domination, security etc.); and cognitive needs (need to plan, learn a skill etc.). This does not mean that information needs are any less important, because success in meeting the one (the primary need) is dependent on meeting the other (information need) and whilst the latter might not be classified as primary, in this increasingly information-dependent age the lack of information could certainly have serious, or even, perilous consequences for the individual. Hence the phrase information-rich and information-poor. Indeed, one could argue that we are moving rapidly to a period of society's development where information has moved to centre stage. The situation is arising where the tail (information) wags the dog (the person or organisation).

The lesson for information professionals in all this is that success in helping people meet their information needs lies in the understanding of the difficulties and problems that give rise to the information need – hence the need for the intermediary to step into their customers' offices and workplaces, join them at coffee breaks, attend their meetings and witness things at first hand. Something that they have often been loathe to do in the past.

Dormant need

People do not always know what their information needs are. They do not know they have an information gap, for they are not aware that there is information out there that could be of help to them. They do not know that new information has rendered obsolete what they know, and, as a result, given rise to another information need. It is only when exposed to the relevant information that the need is recognised. This might be called *dormant need* or *unrecognised need*. Take this case as an example: a person goes down to the photocopying machine to copy a letter. In the queue they overhear a conversation about a television programme screened the previous night, which was about globe artichokes. The person in question eats a lot of globe artichokes so listened with keen interest. The programme claimed that they contained a lot of chemicals because the infrequent rain (in Israel, where they are grown) and the washing process failed to penetrate their tightly closed petals. Now the person did not come to the photocopier with an information need but went away having obtained a needed piece of information. Clearly, in today's world in which information is being generated in ever-increasing volumes and people are being connected to information sources of unparalleled power and reach, such situations must be commonplace, and will increasingly become more commonplace. Information retrieval systems have to take this into account. And there lies the big challenge for them, for, as yet, they have only really concerned themselves with satisfying the direct and specific articulation of information need. The huge popularity of the Internet must be partly due to the fact that it has an unlimited potential to uncover dormant information needs in the searcher. But this comes at some considerable cost.

While the artichoke story is a case of uncovering need by happy accident, users cannot rely on this serendipitous method for all their information. It is too much of a lottery for these information-dependent, knee-jerk times. The uncovering of dormant need has to be put on firmer and surer ground. And this is where information professionals can help. An individual's information need should be best determined in conjunction with information professionals, as they should be best positioned to know what is available and best able to control the information filters, so that exposure to information can be balanced with the problems that arise from information overload. This, of course, creates a positive and proactive role for the information professional: experience and knowledge of information sources and of subjects can point users in the direction of unknown/unthought of material. Of course this is easily said, but less easily done, and it requires trust from the user that only comes from a good and close working relationship.

Unexpressed needs

There is another reason why information needs go unmet, and that is because obstacles and constraints prevent them being met. In these circumstances users are aware of their information needs, but do nothing about them, either because they cannot or will not. With the information bombardment rate set to increase and increase, the number of people failing to express their need is also set to rise similarly spectacularly. The information clinics of the future are likely to be full of people suffering from this complaint.

Information wants

Information wants are what an individual would like to have – *like* being the operative word. In a perfect world information needs and information wants would be the same thing. However, we live in a far from perfect world, and a number of obstacles and factors ensure that not all that is needed is wanted and not all that is wanted is actually needed. We are now moving into a much more subjective domain, where personality, time and resources make themselves felt. Thus individuals may not be motivated to chase information (increasingly because there is too much of it), may not have the time to look for it, have the skills to locate information or, maybe, just do not have access to the necessary information resources (through lack of finance, perhaps). There is a mixture of physical and personal factors at work here. Of course, a price has to be paid if information needs are to be met – time, effort and possibly money has to be expended. Job satisfaction must be a big determinant of whether individuals go ahead and attempt to meet their information needs fully. If you like your job, you will want to do it well, improve it, and keep yourselves up-to-date. This will inevitably mean going out of your way to meet your information needs.

24

Society sends us confusing signals about whether we should want information. On the one hand we are enjoined to sample the joys of the Internet (surely, *the* information-enabling mechanism), the global highway, laptops etc., and on the other hand we have less and less time to enjoy the fruits of this information. And, of course, the things we are enjoined to embrace are also obstacles because they bury us with information.

Questionnaire studies of need typically turn out to be want studies – with questions taking a "would you like more information, more journals, enhanced facilities" line. Results can prove to be very misleading because users happily tick all the want options, happy in the knowledge that they will probably never be required to exercise their options. What happens in practice can turn out to be very different.

Information demands

An information demand is a request for an item of information believed to be wanted. This is where information-seeking starts and the user first encounters the information professional: the user interacts with an information system, source (human or documentary) or intermediary. People may demand information they do not need – someone tells them its a good book, but on receipt it turns out to be a disappointment (lots of information-seeking must lead to blind alleys, especially on the Web) – and they certainly need or want information they do not demand; are not aware that it is there, for instance. Demand is partly dependent on expectation, which in turn depends upon existing information provision. Expectations have generally been low because of users' past contact with traditional libraries: libraries that only ever offered a limited window on information and could never respond within the tight time frames expected by most busy individuals. Furthermore, a poor service from the library or information centre in the past will lower expectations and hence demand (and there is a legacy of poor service in the profession). Many people are unaware of what the information service can do for them so they do not make demands upon it. Computers, however, have raised expectations enormously – users naively believe that these "black boxes" can deliver anything. The Web has raised expectations even more. Even if users are aware of what libraries and information systems can do for them they might still fight shy because interaction with them would expose the user to a reality they would rather not know about – dozens and dozens of items to digest.

Of course, people may want information they do not really need or which is unsuitable – perhaps, their initial perception of its value does not match with reality or, maybe, they just use what is close to hand or what they are aware of. Certainly the Internet stokes up demand and leads inevitably to (very) large amounts of material that is demanded but not needed.

Overall then, information need must be greater than demand, for while relevant information is demanded, there must be a great deal of relevant information that is not sought. Information systems have an important role to play in enabling people to easily and speedily convert needs into wants. Web logs provide an awesome indicator of potential global demand.

Information use

Here we arrive at the more visible end of the information-seeking process – the information the individual actually uses or consumes. This is an area about which information professionals know most, but even here not enough. Use is more than satisfied demand (intended use) for it may also be the result of browsing or accidental discovery (while not looking purposively for anything or when looking for something else). The term *unintended use* is sometimes used to cover browsing and accidental discovery of information, but, of course, browsing can be much more directed and structured than that. Some people browse because they have no choice, because they cannot recognise and articulate their need until something they see reminds them of it. Some people browse because they are forced to do so because of the way the information system – the Web, for instance – displays the information. In the case of oral information the amount and proportion of information gathered without being directly sought must be very, very high indeed. Indeed, this is probably true of a good deal of information-seeking in the social sciences as well.

The difference between intended use and unintended use is an important one in terms of information system design, and consequently usage studies should attempt to distinguish between the two forms.

As people can only use what is available use is very heavily dependent upon provision and access. In theory, the more information that is accessible the more it is likely to be used – we could call this the Web phenomenon. Indeed, exposing users to information is an important task for the information professional. With increased pressures on people that arise from the wall-to-wall communication and real-time information world we live in, this does have to be done with great care. There is a strong risk of overloading people.

Use, of course, is a word that comes with a lot of baggage. It is not the clean, hard, direct manifestation of need that some seem to suppose. Firstly, different levels or depths of use can be distinguished. The first level of use simply involves determining whether something is worth using in the first place. That use may satisfy or fail to satisfy need. Use and satisfaction do not always go hand-in-hand. Transaction log analyses typically measure this type of use. The second level is the use or consumption of information that is determined as being relevant (citation studies generally measure this type of use). In either case use might also lead to other people being alerted to the potential worth of the information consumed. Secondly, there is the problem of how we recognise use – what indicators do we employ, for use has many recorded manifestations. We have already mentioned citations and logs and there are also library issue statistics, book sales records and the ubiquitous tick boxes in questionnaires that ask users whether they used the information system daily, weekly, monthly etc. (mysteriously, always assuming that information use is a rhythmic or periodic activity). Plainly many of these use indicators are measuring different things.

As previously mentioned it is argued that use data are very valuable as they point most directly to the needs experienced by people. Clearly use can be a manifestation of need and in perfect circumstances it might be fully equated with it. Of course, bean (use) counting does come stripped of the wish-list or fantasy factor that is so endemic of questionnaire surveys, and that is an undoubted advantage. What really makes use data especially attractive to many information professionals is that it is generally to hand and there is lots of it.

The real problem associated with use data shows itself best in connection with the Internet. Just consider what constitutes use on the Web and what can be read into it. For use on the Web read 'visits' or pages viewed ('hits'). Putting aside the problems of actually determining this – something we shall return to in the methodology section, let's try and establish what, say, pages viewed really signifies. For a start, with the loose and idiosyncratic method of searching on the Web and the shotgun approach of most search engines to retrieval, the chances that you actually want to see that page you end up with has to be low. However, you 'used' it and you are recorded on the logs as having done so, and action will be taken by others – advertisers, sponsors, and web managers, on the basis of this data. Furthermore, how many times do you navigate through a site, going down numerous pathways to get what you really want? Each page you go through on your way to the page you really need is another page 'used' but not needed. The irony, of course, is that use data has never been such an important measure – how else can sites measure their effectiveness and whether the investment was worth it: that is why site managers constantly bang-on about hits or visits. But it is counterfeit currency, it really is very unreliable. Those who say that, at the very least, use is a concrete measure should think again.

Use data must be handled with care as it is a crude indicator of need. It is surely only on the basis of information needs data that effective information services can be built. It often turns out that studies claiming to be investigating needs are in fact looking at nothing other than use or demand – data which is much closer to hand or easier to collect. Citation and library loan studies are frequently guilty here of playing the needs card. But as we have already seen information need is, in theory, greater than use plus demand. Use and demand data can help an information system improve on what it is already doing, but there is no guarantee that it was on the right lines in the first place: they will not help build a system which will do new things. And, of course, in the case of use studies – especially library use studies, non-users – often a disturbingly large number of the population, are not taken into the equation. Non-users may not only be in the majority – and users form a small self-selecting group, but they might also prove to be a more financially attractive group. We know, for instance, that senior managers have traditionally been the ones that have shied away from using information systems.

User (or I-player)

Before we leave the topic of use let us consider the term user itself. The word is generally used inaccurately for often it is used to describe non-users, too. The population being described by the term is an ideal one, a potential one, and an inclusive one. Essentially it is used to describe someone who might avail himself or herself of an information service. There are some hidden assumptions here that tell us a lot about the profession's psyche. The first assumption is that it covers most people – but frequently it does not. Despite the hype, Internet users still do not constitute the majority of the population. The second assumption is that it is good to use. And this explains the evangelical approach of many information professionals towards their 'flock'. The implication is that use is *the* normal state, but this is not always the case. There is really no word that means one who has a need.

There is a more general complaint that can be levelled at the word. User (and users), like information, has lost much of its meaning. It is a tired, over-used, cheap and misused word, which provides the information profession with a debased currency. It no longer reflects the close and complex engagement that takes place between a person and today's interactive information systems. The word "users" paints a picture of a featureless mass, a lumpen proletariat, a homogenous body – people who are accustomed to being fed information in batch-processing mode (Fifties-style). It is too passive and too mechanical for today's information environment. It does not recognise the fact that digital information systems create much greater information diversity than print-based systems. It also fails to convey that today's 'user' has to be fleet of foot to succeed in these fast-changing times. Basically it is the wrong word, in the wrong place, at the wrong time.

What we really need is a more active and accurate term. *Information player* could be that term; *player* used in the context of sport, meaning a football or cricket player, or in the context or business, meaning someone who invests in financial markets. *I-player* would appear to be a powerful abbreviation. It is a term much richer in meaning, one that conveys action and individuality. It is a term that recognises that today's information-seeking can be interactive, recreational, social and competitive.

- *Interactive*. Today's user plays a much more important, complicated, creative and engaged role in the information-seeking process. The term user is one-dimensional and, if dynamic at all, that is only in a linear sense. Player on the other hand suggests a multidimensional evolving relationship – the kind of relationship that is so much a feature of modern day information systems, like the Web. A player is constantly looking for new routes to goal – evaluating options (information) as they go. The player is part of the system while the user is someone who stands outside the system, looking in. Players operate in an information space (cyberspace) while users use information systems.

- *Recreational.* Today's information systems are now very much an extension of our real life – and this will prove to be even more so as the digital mobile phone expands its horizons into the information retrieval domain. The word player comes from the real world whereas the term user is more of a theoretical construction. Information-seeking today is no longer just about professional problem solving; it can be recreational (and mindless) too[3]. Indeed, the distinction between the two in the serendipitous and supermarket environment of the Web is increasingly blurred. In a sense this has been partly recognised through the use of the term surfing (for information), but this word is rather too shallow a description for the process.

- *Social.* Information gathering is a social activity. The social context of the term is very important. Players play with somebody else. Players have different social roles: you have, for instance, teacher and student, politician and voter, journalist and reader.

- *Competitive.* There are costs – financial and/or time costs, associated with finding – or not finding – information. You can win or lose in the information-chasing game. Players can be seen as information investors.

The word player has other important connotations. Firstly, it is a term that acknowledges the economic and political realities of the new millennium. There has been a shift in power from information producer to information consumer. The information consumer now holds centre stage. This fact worries academic librarians and Media moguls alike. Indeed, anyone who manages large, centralised, inflexible batch-processing-style information factories. Today's consumers have a wide choice and can quickly vote with their feet (mice?).

Secondly, the word player is closely connected with the term spectacle. This is very important because the Internet is the biggest capitalistic spectacle of our times. Witness how people pay fortunes for impressive Internet addresses. Witness the amazing rise of e-commerce. There are fortunes to be had for the big players and games and adventures for the not so lucky. We are both actors in, and audience of, the spectacle.

Thirdly, the term player is very much an Internet-type word. The Internet is very much part of the liberal world economy – the word "user" most certainly is not, but player most definitely is. There is a pressing need to get our words in line with the vocabulary of the Internet. The Internet has its own rich and picturesque language for describing itself. We cannot ignore this. It is only by employing this language that information professionals can address the much larger information audience that the Internet commands. We are dealing with post-modernist reality. The first goal of a new language is to facilitate narrative discourse. In a post-modernist world it is discourse which creates and legalises vocabulary. Discourse also constitutes a research activity.

The concept of a player is helpful in understanding how people interact with information systems – and re-visiting what we have said and learnt about them in the past. Continuing the sports analogy, few goals are probably scored in a textbook manner. In any football game players do a lot of things that are not in the training/coaching manuals. Similarly, a lot of information is collected by unconventional or serendipitous means. Thus, maybe, what we first saw as minimalist and idiosyncratic information behaviour was not so odd or strange after all. Using the player concept helps us to get a better understanding of what the logs – and what we, witness at the terminal, PC, or mobile phone.

References

3. Research has shown that peak use of web sites is at office lunch times. Nicholas, D and Huntington, P. Who uses Web newspapers, how much and for what? A log analysis of The Times/Sunday Times web sites. *NetMedia99 Conference: Proceedings*. City University, July 1999.

4. A Framework for Evaluating Information Needs

If information needs data are to be routinely employed in the working environment then there is a requirement to place the slippery concept of information need in a comprehensive, precise and understandable analytical framework. An evaluatory framework that can be profitably used at both a macro level – for effective strategic information management planning, and at a micro level – for the efficient carrying out of routine enquiry work and on-line searching. Its key function is to bring the user to their rightful place at the forefront of the information chain; but above all else it should insure that information delivery is targeted and relevant. Also, implicit in the form of the analysis, is that information needs are highly personal, varying even amongst those doing the same work in the same organisation. Indeed, this very fact is responsible for some information professionals shying away from studying need in the first place – they worry about the variability and dynamic nature of the data and what sense they can make of it. The traditional type of need (user) survey – like citation studies – have concentrated on building stereotypes of user behaviour and it is questionable whether, outside of research science, any of these stereotypes exist in the real world, although the myths perpetuated by these studies fuel professional practice.

More specifically the analytical framework can be used:

- to benchmark the needs of a chosen information communities and make comparisons between them;

- to monitor and evaluate the effectiveness and appropriateness of existing information systems from a user perspective – an essential part of the wider information audit that many commentators have called for (Webb, 1994);

- to detect gaps in information service provision and to remain vigilant to changes in need;

- in the designing of on-going information support system for the individual (personalised information services). It is the key to the provision of bespoke information and the only realistic response to overload – the bet noire of the information world. Selective Dissemination of Information Services (SDI) and push/pull technology have to take their lead from personal information needs assessments;

- in the assessment of the never-ending tide of new information products;

- to ensure that the reference interview, an essential part of the delegation process, is conducted on a firm footing and in a systematic and comprehensive manner;

- to bring the user and the information professional closer together – the questioning and monitoring process that underpins the methodology itself will ensure this.

It is far more difficult attempting to describe the characteristics of information need than other needs, like that for housing, for instance. This is probably partly to do with the fact that information is a less concrete and more diffuse subject, although arguably with media, communications, IT and, now, the Internet, featuring so strongly in the daily news – and in people's daily lives, it is getting much less so. It also stems from the fact that information needs arise from other needs and thus obtain far less individual thought and consideration from people, and, as a result, its characteristics are not so easily remembered or disentangled. But, just as you can describe the key characteristics of housing need as being: building material, site location, type (apartment, semi-detached), number of rooms, architectural design/character, and age/period of the property, so too can the characteristics of information need be described.

It is possible to identify eleven major characteristics of information need: subject, function, nature, intellectual level, viewpoint, quantity, quality/authority, date/currency, speed of delivery, place of publication/origin, and processing and packaging. A few of these, like subject and language, are familiar to all information professionals, but most, unfortunately, are not – and they are by no means the minor characteristics. So not only is there a problem of getting people to conduct needs studies in the first place, but, even when they do them, there is the problem of getting them to do it comprehensively.

Subject

Subject is probably the most obvious and immediate characteristic of information need. After all most libraries arrange their document collections by subject. In some respects it is an imposed characteristic. While it is undoubtedly a very important characteristic of need – central to nearly all information need statements – the trouble is that, too often, information professionals expect information need to be described in subject terms alone. In today's hurried times it is all too easy to translate everything into the ubiquitous keyword. Indeed, there are machines that will do this for you. It is easy to see how this comes about: users are coached to couch their requests in subject terms – albeit more expansively than most systems can deal with, and information professionals ask for subject terms (keywords) in return so that they can search their information systems – access to information systems is universally provided by subject. Even when alternative access points are provided they are often overlooked in the headlong rush to find the most appropriate keyword. The portrayal of information need through keywords alone is symptomatic of the shallow thinking that surrounds the subject. Subject keywords provide the quick fix – although, of course, they fix very little as every user of a Web search engine is only too aware. It also keeps the information exchange between intermediary and client (artificially) short, which is – it is alleged –

what the client wants, but this surely is not the place to hurry or skimp. Everything flows from the accurate and comprehensive analysis of need – it is the very cornerstone of the delegation process.

Having said all that, there have been occasions when information system designers have not accorded the subject approach sufficient attention. Designers of early-computerised bibliographic systems, like OPACs, were particularly guilty of marginalising the subject searcher and exaggerating the importance of the author/title searcher. Thus subject was not even on the first search options screen of the Parliamentary on-line information service (POLIS), when it was introduced in the late Eighties.

There are a number of characteristics connected with subject description that need consideration:

(1) the number of subjects involved;
(2) the depth in which these subjects are to be pursued;
(3) the problems associated with specification.

The number of subjects of interest

This is of particular concern to the running of current awareness and SDI services. In such cases it is necessary to determine how many, and what subjects, are required. Few people are in the lucky position of having to know only about one thing – most undertake a number of roles, each with its own subject requirements. Just on the job front alone an individual might function in a number of capacities. Thus a university lecturer might have teaching, counselling, research, consultancy, administrative, professional and union responsibilities. In today's multidisciplinary and multitasking world the number of subjects that people are expected to keep in touch with is forever on the increase. It is all too easy to service what is thought to be the individual's lead role, yet we should not jump to the conclusion that this is where the most pressing need for information is. Indeed, it could be argued, that the individual would already have ensured that arrangements were satisfactory in this department, and it is elsewhere – outside the mainstream interest – where help is needed.

People's interests and responsibilities change – nothing is set in concrete. So routine and regular monitoring of the subject premises upon which information systems are built must be carried out if they are to maintain their effectiveness. Virus-checking programs today often update their scanning lists daily and intermediaries should take their lead from them. Updating needs profiles or passports should be conducted at the very least once every six months to maintain their effectiveness. Once a quarter is better.

Specificity or depth of interest

There is also the question of how deep lies the interest, or how specific is the request. Suppose a user was interested in organic gardening, would they require general information – *The manual of organic gardening*, for instance, or everything that falls within the compass of the term, including such detailed items as *The no-digging approach to potato*

41

cultivation. Get it wrong and you have made a huge mistake, either unleashing a flood of dense information on the unwary, or choking off the supply of information to the needy. What makes the whole matter rather tricky is the fact that most people's jobs require them to have a detailed knowledge on some things and a broader understanding of many other things. Of course, they know which requires what treatment, but does the intermediary or system know? This has to be untangled at the outset. Take the example of a Library School lecturer. Their prime teaching interest – on which they spend most of their time, and have done so for many years – is on-line searching. It follows that, as one of the systems they teach is Dialog, you could alert them to everything newly written about Dialog and they would be grateful. However, the same lecturer must also keep in touch with events in the broader Library world for they are training students to work in libraries. The need here though, is for general, contextual data or information on key professional events only: a general item on the financial problems faced by public libraries would be acceptable, but, perhaps, only one item, and not too detailed at that. In the rush to meet specific and immediate information needs, the need for general professional information is easily overlooked and yet, users rate this type of data very highly.

Obstacles to subject specification

There are a number of problems associated with defining the subject of information need:

1. the generalisation or simplification of the subject request by the client;

2. the vagueness with which the client describes the subject;

3. the problems encountered by both client and intermediary in translating the user's keywords into those employed by the information systems.

Generalising the subject request

People, in their attempt to communicate to the intermediary the subject of their concern, frequently generalise the query. They do this for a number of reasons. The principal one is to allow the intermediary to enter the dialogue gently: to enable them to come in at the shallow end, to ease their way in to what the person considers to be a complicated and intractable problem that they have spent a long time considering, but to whom the intermediary comes cold. There are other reasons for generalising the query:

• the intermediary is not necessarily a subject expert so the person generalises to simplify things for them;

• the person is not aware of what the intermediary can offer, so to minimise this risk of early rejection, and to provide space for negotiation, they generalise the request;

• a shortage of time and the desire to get a prompt reply leads to an abbreviation of the request.

Every information worker must have his or her own pet examples of hopelessly general questions. The author's own gem occurred whilst working as a readers' adviser in a busy public library: the request was for books on fish. Now in a public library there are books on catching fish, cooking fish, the biology of fish and fish as pets, to name just the most obvious possibilities. After further questioning it transpired that it was the biology of fish that was needed. Take, too, this real-life on-line query: *I wonder if there is any information on new cars* [on the system]. The actual requirement was for dealers' prices for the Honda Civic.

Vague subject descriptions

Closely related to general question-framing is vague question-framing – sometimes the two are indistinguishable. Confidentiality concerns can lead the person to cloak or camouflage their interest from the intermediary, so that others are not alerted to their particular line of enquiry. This can happen in newspaper libraries, and especially in those that serve journalists from a number of papers, as is the case at News International and the Mirror Group. More often vague subject specification mirrors the users' own confusion and uncertainty as to what they want: it is difficult for them to verbalise their own problem, although they will recognise what they want when they see it. After all, users are asking for information to fill a gap in their own knowledge: plainly, this must inevitably lead to some imprecision in the formulation of the query.

Problems of translating user-generated keywords into the language of the information system

Here lies the big challenge – and the graveyard of many information needs profiles. Outside the pure sciences you would be lucky to find a coincidence between the subject terms supplied by the client to describe their needs and the subject terms used by information systems or authors to describe the documents that the client might find interesting. In the multidisciplinary, dynamic, and fashion-affected fields of the social sciences this can prove particularly problematical – loose, ill-defined and shifting terminology makes subject specification both difficult and transitory. Two examples help to illustrate the nature of the problem. A research academic requested a watching brief to be kept on material published on the topic of people doing work on the side i.e. without the various government authorities knowing. The academic provides the intermediary with the term *moonlighting*. However, a comprehensive trawl of the literature would soon uncover more terms – *second economy, underground economy; black economy; black market*. All of these terms will have to be employed, if the search is not to become a lottery. A search for material on the *elderly* – a relatively simple concept one might have thought – is, in fact, even more problematical with the following possible alternatives: *retired people, old age, the aged, senior citizens, pensioners, old people, old persons*. It gets much more complicated than this when two or more concepts are involved.

The lessons that need be learned here are these:

- people are unlikely to furnish all the terms the information system needs for it to produce the goods;
- people are unlikely – even when prodded (by pop-up boxes, for instance) – to provide the most productive terms;
- the information professional will have to spend some time scanning thesauri and sample issues of secondary services to come up with sufficient terms to adequately clothe the subject – and even then they will have to undertake pilot searches to test the validity of these terms and discover natural language equivalents.

After all this has been done it will still be necessary to monitor the products of these terms to ensure fine-tuning of the subject profile. Thesauri are extremely important tools in these deliberations – and, ideally, should be consulted in the presence of the customer (the broad-narrow and related term networks provide them with an excellent word map in which to place their topic). Of course, it goes without saying that it is unlikely that there will be a consensus amongst the thesauri consulted.

Function (use to which the information is put)

Each individual and each information community puts information to work in different ways. Their end products are different and so are their uses for information. In the case of the journalist information is used to write stories, in the case of the social worker it often used to answer resource questions concerning their clients, and in the case of academics it will be used to help compile a lecture or update a reading list. Within each profession (and organisation) the prime function to which information is put will vary according to the role and specialism of the individual. Thus managers in social work departments would be using information to monitor the progress of the organisation, rather than to answer the resource questions of the client group. There are, however, some generalisations that can be made about the functions to which people put information. Essentially, people need information for five broad functions or purposes, and it is very important to distinguish between them for they require very different information solutions. The five are: (1) providing answers to specific questions (the fact-finding function); (2) to keep up-to-date (the current awareness function); (3) the investigation of a new field in-depth (the research function); (4) to obtain a background understanding of an issue/topic (the briefing function); and (5) to provide ideas or a stimulus (the stimulus function).

The fact-finding function

Firstly, people need information to obtain answers to specific questions. These questions are familiar to all reference librarians: they are of the 'who, why, what, where, when and how' kind. Such questions may be simple, like the address of an organisation or individual, a biographical portrait; or complex, like the number of aircraft near-misses that occurred in 1987. Everybody has this need and for most of us it is a frequent, perhaps, everyday need. Huge sales of such fact-finding tools as Whitakers Almanac, The Statesman's Yearbook and Encarta bear testament to the strength of the need amongst end-users. There is a lot of evidence to suggest that the Web is used in this way – as a giant encyclopaedia and telephone directory. The need is relatively precise and well-defined and is generally met by facts, names, addresses, statistics, and the like. It is probably true to say that for practitioners this is the dominant information function – many of the resource queries made by social workers fall into this camp. Not a lot of information is involved in meeting this type of need and the interchange between user and information system/intermediary is consequently brief: therefore, such needs are generally easily and cheaply met. They are also easily delegated.

The current awareness function

There is the need to keep up-to-date. This is also a generally widely-felt need, but in some fields and professions the concern is much more pressing. In dynamic fields, which are characterised by sudden, frequent and widespread change, then maintaining a hold on what is going on is an essential part of professionalism. This is plainly the case with all journalists and enormous amounts of money are spent assembling complex information systems to enable them to do this. In academia, too, professionalism is associated with keeping up-to-date, but here it is with research rather than events. Practitioners have frequently been singled out for criticism by researchers on the grounds that they fail to keep up-to-date, but really this charge is associated with a failure to keep up-to-date with the literature and not the issues.

Keeping up-to-date causes problems, because to do so effectively, requires close support from (computerised) information systems, for only they can systematically monitor the enormous amount of information that is typically involved. A greater expenditure of time and effort on the part of the individual is required, because more data is involved – not all of it of immediate relevance – and this means a lot of time spent on vetting and digesting the data. Current awareness need is inevitably vaguer than the need for facts. Therefore it is an information activity that is sometimes put on the back burner, dropped or conveniently overlooked. Also, whereas fact-finding is usually associated with immediate and often urgent problem-solving – and hence has to be dealt with speedily, this is not the case with current awareness. There is often no direct pay-off – the effect is much more long term. With increasing time and resource pressures at most workplaces there is much anecdotal evidence to suggest that people are not keeping up-to-date as they once did. It is probably here that information systems can provide the greatest help, mainly by prioritising, filtering and sorting through the data.

The research function

Researching a new field in depth is a far less frequent and widespread concern. Most people have the need to do this only a few dozen times in their lives, but with changing work practices, a need for a more multi-skilled and mobile workforce, life-long learning and the rapid growth in the numbers of students doing dissertations and projects; the approach is on the increase. By definition those in research and academe are the most likely to need information for this purpose. Whilst computerised information systems make the retrieval and archival side of things much easier, the time required to evaluate and absorb the resultant data is enormous – and constitutes the major information problem. Indeed, because computerised systems can find more information more quickly, it can be argued that, in some ways, they have made matters worse. Because of the sheer volume of information usually involved, the large costs associated with retrieving the data (the combined connect and display charges levied by many on-line hosts will ensure that), and the time-demands on the user (especially in connection with the Web), it is essential to establish beforehand that the need for comprehensiveness and exhaustiveness that is so characteristic of the research need is really what is required. The novice or naive intermediary too readily associate all requests for information to be of this kind, for they confuse a good search with a big search – and none come bigger than those associated with the research need – a marvellous opportunity to demonstrate their prowess.

Do not confuse a fact-requiring question for a research one, because the information outcomes are as different as they can be. The trouble is that, because so much information science teaching and research concerns academics – they commend themselves because they are a pliant and orderly group to which they can relate, students come away with a stereotype of information need, which they believe applies to the population as a whole. The consequence of this is that when they come to work in a practitioner environment they adopt information solutions more appropriate to academic information problems. And that is when the fun starts.

The briefing/background function

Not everyone has the time or need to research a field in depth, though many people need a briefing on topics with which they are broadly familiar, but perhaps insufficiently acquainted with the detail, and briefly and fleetingly need to be. Generally, the broader the subject interest and the less time available, the greater the need for the background brief. Journalists, caught between the need to say something authoritative about almost anything and with very little notice or time to do this, are great practitioners of the background search – cuttings traditionally fulfil this need. Politicians, too, are expected to have a view on anything, so it is not surprising to discover that one of their preferred information forms are the background papers produced by The House of Commons Library. These are two good examples of information professionals anticipating information needs. This is another area where information professionals can really bring their skills to bear. Probably, for most users, newspapers perform a key briefing function.

The greater the information flow the greater and more widespread the need for briefing. Ironically the Web – the chief culprit for the information deluge we are experiencing, is a great briefing source.

The stimulus function

In the cases of all the other functions people generally know what they are looking for, though the levels of specificity and definition vary somewhat. However, in this particular case the user has only the vaguest idea of what they are looking for – and sometimes no idea at all. Indeed, they interact with information sources and systems in the hope that this will result in them finding out what they need. By seeing something that they don't want they are perversely alerted to something they do want. Because the searching associated with this particular need is inevitably unfocused and unstructured, intermediaries who observe it are often led to the mistaken belief that what they are witnessing is poor searching. Much of the rubbishing of end-users' searching skills found in the professional literature results from a poor understanding of the characteristic information-seeking behaviour that results from individuals trying to meet this kind of need. It is through exposure to large datasets that users discover what they want: it is doubtful whether stimulation can be obtained with small sets of data. There is some evidence to suggest that Web search engines and full-text databases, with their idiosyncratic natural language indexing, can actually boost the stimulus effect, by providing unusual and unexpected associations of documents. Of course, what is meant to stimulate can also irritate – and a situation in which the individual is overloaded is all too easy achieved.

One of the reasons why people do not delegate the search is that they believe that information professionals will not be able to recognise what will be of value to them. But if they asked more about the function to which the information is to be put they would have a far better idea. Intermediaries are sometimes hesitant to ask such questions in the mistaken belief that this constitutes a form of prying – something which has never worried the doctor, teacher or lawyer: it is as much a matter of confidence and professionalism as anything else.

Nature

There is not an ideal label for this information needs characteristic. A clearer idea of what is involved can be obtained through listing the various types of information that fall within its compass. What is at the heart of the matter is whether it is conceptual or theoretical, historical, descriptive, statistical or methodological information that is required. Plainly there are differences here – and big ones at that. In any subject information will be found produced in all these forms – and, importantly, some of these forms will prove to be highly unpalatable to some people. Nature, like level, is very much allied to the readership/audience for whom the information is intended. Thus social science practitioners, for instance, will hardly ever require their information produced in a theoretical manner or from a historical point of view – though their academic colleagues most probably would.

On the whole, theoretical information has a very limited circulation. Much more the province of the practitioner in all fields, is descriptive, methodological and statistical data. Consumers might reject almost all forms other than descriptive and historical forms. The need for methodological information cuts across the academic/practitioner divide, being required by practitioners such as teachers, engineers and social workers and by research scientists of all kinds. If we interpret the term widely to mean 'how to do' information then hobbyists of all types would be interested in this type of information.

Traditionally the designers of information systems have neglected this information characteristic. Few systems provide for retrieval along these lines although a number offer access to statistical accounts (like the Parliamentary on-line information system – POLIS) and the British National Bibliography once offered a wide degree of access through its PRECIS indexing system.

Intellectual level/level of complexity

This characteristic refers to the minimum extent of knowledge and sometimes the level of intelligence of the individual in order to understand the information. It is all to do with the intelligibility or otherwise of information. Information is made complex not just by how much knowledge and education it assumes but also by how abstract or compressed it is. Writing styles and skills do count here too; after all, some broadsheet newspapers deal with some very complex ideas but these articles are made intelligible by excellent processing and packaging of the data. It is not simply a question of matching the intellectual powers of individuals with suitably intellectual documents, because intellectually advanced individuals might require elementary knowledge in a related or marginal field. Thus a research scientist coming to grips with spreadsheets for the first time could be on the same information footing as the school secretary. Having said that, however, it is probably true to say that a novice will generally not require intellectually advanced information.

There is a danger that things can become too simplistic. Between the advanced user and the elementary user, and between advanced information and elementary information, there is a huge spread of values – getting the pitch right requires a lot of fine-tuning. In an effort to meet the requirement for suitably written material, some information systems index documents according to their intellectual level. Thus ERIC allocates academic/research, practitioner and consumer codes to documents to assist with their digestion. It is well-documented in the social sciences that practitioners will on the whole never read the academic/research literature of their fields; however, in the sciences the literatures are not so mutually exclusive and thus in Medicine we would find GPs reading research, albeit, through their own journals, such as *The British Medical Journal* and *The Lancet*.

Journalists play an important role in making the contents of academic reports and research accessible to a much wider public. Thus the medical correspondents of broadsheet newspapers, like *The Guardian* and *The Independent*, regularly repackage articles from *The Lancet* or *British Journal of Medicine* for an essentially popular audience. This topic is taken up in more detail in the Processing and packaging section.

There has been much debate over whether information and communication are being increasingly 'dumbed' down. The dumbing down is alleged to result from too much information/communication, too little time to absorb it and a tendency on technology's part to treat the individual as a voyeur. More information sometimes means less knowledge. There is a worry – especially in the Media, that news is being dumbed down by 24 hours of news bombardment from a vast array of channels, where currency and immediacy take precedence over detail and analysis. There is a real fear of a world full of 'information malnutrition', where people are simply unable to digest information. The result of so many news and information channels coming on to the market, courtesy of the Web, is fast and fleeting information.

Viewpoint

Information, especially in the social science and life style fields, is sometimes written up from a particular point of view, approach or angle and consumers may require information sympathetic to the views that they subscribe to. This is probably most commonly seen in newspaper readership, where people like to subscribe to newspapers presenting news and views from their own political and social standpoint. Information on the same topic, but written up from a different point of view or slant would be unpalatable to many people. This is one needs characteristic that really gets people worked up. Because there are so many different approaches to writing up information it is helpful to categorise and further distinguish between them: there is school of thought, political orientation, positive or negative approaches and, in interdisciplinary fields, discipline orientation.

School of thought

Schools of thought are most evident in the social sciences, where they abound. The best known schools are probably feminism, Marxism and monetarism, but there are many others. Feminism and Marxism also help shape information in the humanities. The humanities have their own schools of course, like neo-classicism/modernism in architecture and structuralism in literature. These schools are large, widely known and have handy labels to describe them, but there are countless mini-schools or 'departments', which inhabit nearly all disciplines. In the field of information studies, for instance, we have the systems-driven and user-driven schools of thought. It is at this rather more specific level that it is possible to discern schools of thought in science. These mostly concern themselves with ethical considerations, like abortion and animal-testing, although Professor Leaky, the food poisoning expert from Leeds University, shows that even in mainstream science writers may differ fundamentally in their interpretation of events. Some sceptics believe that the consensus in science arises from scientists agreeing not to disagree! It was once thought that in scientific fields information did not fragment itself in the way that it does in some social science disciplines, like Politics or Sociology. However, the recent and ongoing intellectual battles over genetically modified food, BSE and organic farming techniques are every bit as heated and polarised as they are in the social sciences.

A major problem with catering for school of thought in information needs profiles is that authors – founding fathers and key disciples aside – do not normally identify which, if any, school they are writing from. Some information systems help by providing viewpoint indexing – the British National Bibliography did so for a time with its PRECIS system – but this help is generally limited. Often the best method of obtaining usable viewpoint data is by asking clients for authors that they 'follow'. These names can then be supplemented by identifying related authors through an examination of citation indexes, though this can prove risky with academics, as they are often fond of denouncing their immediate rivals (in an attempt to boost their own academic standing). Possibly, the organisation the person works for is the best guide. Thus, when it comes to organic farming we know clearly where the Soil Association and the National Union of Farmers stand.

Political orientation

It is also in the social sciences that we see information written up consistently from a political point of view: there are right-wing, left-wing, conservative, socialist points of view – to name the most obvious. Of course, school of thought and political orientation may coincide. It would be difficult, for instance, to characterise the pro- and anti-European stance that drives much of today's politics in the UK.

While people feel more comfortable with, and more disposed towards, reading information sympathetic to their own political allegiances, it would be wrong to assume that they would not be interested in information emanating from a different political persuasion. Thus politicians will often scan the opposition parties' newspapers, hoping that they can use something there as ammunition to throw at the opposition in debate or interview. A quote from *The Guardian* used by a Conservative politician in the debating chamber can prove most telling.

As with school of thought, the political standpoint of information is not always easily discerned, except when it comes from a mainstream political party, of course. Little help can be expected from the available information systems, so if this need is to be met, it can prove a long and costly exercise. There are, however, shortcuts. Thus many organisations are associated with a political point of view. And we are not just talking about political parties – think tanks, research centres/organisations, associations, unions, voluntary/pressure groups, governments, newspapers and, even, university departments can be associated with a political point of view. A document on the environment by the Automobile Association is likely to differ fundamentally in tone from one issued by The Friends of the Earth, for instance. So obtaining lists of suitably-minded organisations can help a lot in the meeting the need for information shaped by political considerations. Corporate authors are too often left off user needs' specifications.

Information professionals, especially those in the public service, have sometimes fought shy of providing information presented from a political point of view, believing that this compromises them in some way. However, more often than not, it is more of a case of them not being sympathetic to the political stand being avowed. Of course, this is naive in the first instance and almost a form of Big Brotherism in the second instance. There can be nothing wrong with providing information in this manner. Indeed, at the House of Commons, where the Library has to walk a political tightrope, librarians frequently prompt the inquirer as to what political end the data is required for. That way the information can be used to its best advantage. If they of all people have no qualms about this, why should anyone else?

Positive/negative approaches

There is a need for information to be presented in a positive or negative form – as the existence of 'spin doctors' confirms. Catering for this need has also proved controversial and challenging for information professionals. Library students are particularly aghast when told that this is a legitimate characteristic of information need. The demand is greatest amongst those in politics, the media and business. No doubt if more information systems catered for this approach the demand would be even greater. Both the Labour and Conservative parties in the UK have, what they call *dirt* databases on individual MPs, upon which they keep unsavoury stories, injudicious quotes, incidences of poor behaviour, voting inconsistencies – all data to be leaked or exposed at a suitably telling time, e.g. a media interview with an opposing politician. The need for this type of data is best shown in an enquiry the author conducted for a national newspaper. A prominent politician was suing the newspaper over something they had said he had said, but he said he hadn't. The quote made the politician look bad and he wanted them to retract it. For the newspaper the best defence was to get the *dirt* on this politician and show that in the past he had said things which he had later denied, proving that his memory/word could not be relied upon.

Who would deny that this is an important and valid information need, yet few information professionals would/could field it. Certainly dirt in this context is unlikely to feature as a database keyword, and political databases, like POLIS, are obviously going to be unhelpful here. Far better to try publications that are only ever going to show this politician or personality in a bad light – *Private Eye* and some biographies, for instance. Or perhaps, go to a politically motivated organisation that is opposed to his or her political views. Possibly, negative information is most commonly obtained by users through oral and informal channels of communication, but to have its greatest impact it needs to be documented.

Today the Web is the best peddler of 'documented' dirt information. The Drudge Report political site is a case in point. There is a strong demand for the controversial, gossip and plain dirt and the Web meets much of this need. The fact that the Internet contains information of dubious, but interesting, quality is a plus, especially for journalists. In particular features journalists and those charged with producing articles of unusual "human interest" or of a generally lighter nature tend, as might be expected, to be most interested. Indeed, in a lot of cases they are looking for information and angles regardless of its authenticity.

Subject orientation

In interdisciplinary fields where authors and information providers possess a number of different subject backgrounds, there is the need to consider the subject orientation of the information requirement. Criminology provides a good illustration of this. University criminology departments are staffed by academics who approach the subject from a wide range of disciplines. Thus, for instance, the criminology department of Middlesex University studies criminology from the perspective of sociology; whereas the academics at Manchester University study criminology from a psychological perspective and those of Cambridge University from the standpoint of law. Any assessment of the information needs of criminologists must take this into account.

Of course, the information requirement may be the very opposite of what has been described above. Users may actually want information that is wholly objective. The objectivity of the information producer/source is very important to bureaucrats in their use of information. This would be true of scientists too.

Quantity

While every one requires a certain amount of information to do a job or solve a problem, the size of the information appetite varies greatly, not only between individuals and groups, but also according to the nature of the need. Modern society requires us to be more informed than ever before – the enormous pressures created by rapid change and the march of computerisation ensures that. Increasing performance monitoring and the call for greater competitiveness in all walks of life play their part too. The very presence of vast quantities of data in every form provides its own form of encouragement as well. Hence, the attraction of the Web. Motivation, diligence and the amount of time available to digest information are all influential factors in determining the amount of information consumed. Something else which is influential, is the fact that, in recent times, we have all moved from a situation where the main information problem was getting hold of information, to a situation where the chief problem is digesting (or avoiding) the information that all too easily flows our way. So this information characteristic is unusual in that it can also be an information constraint.

A researcher starting out on a new subject field might want all the information they can lay their hands on, as would probably someone starting a new job. An investigative journalist embarking on a new story might think similarly. Thus the request to *give me everything you've got on ...* is far from uncommon in journalist-information worker exchanges, and more than one journalist interviewed by the author actually said that *you can't have too much information*. Far from a cause for concern the volume of information may be thought to be a cause for celebration, regardless of any retrieval problems: *There is a fantastic amount of information available ... you can access wires, you access libraries, you access information all around the world ... in an office ... or at home ... it is quite fantastic.*

But most people do not have the time, inclination or need to wade through large volumes of information – they would in the main be content to have sufficient, but small quantities, of information. To reach this end they would sample (choosing the best) or even information gamble (taking a chance on what comes to hand). Indeed, the real problem for most people is that they are inundated with information and they have little chance of getting through it. It is, of course, a mistake to assume that more information increases knowledge: rather like food consumption, after a while it does you more harm than good. Similarly, it would be wrong to believe that there is always something essentially important about getting (more) information. Take, for instance, this quote from a respondent in the Information Requirements of Social Scientists research project (Bath University, 1971). *The impor-*

tance of information can be overrated. More information does not always result in increased knowledge and probably seldom produces increased wisdom. Now this was said some thirty years ago, although it is even more pertinent today. It is mostly in regard to the volume of information required that information professionals get information needs requirements wrong. Too many judge their own information prowess by the amount of information that they can provide in response to an enquiry. A long list or bibliography is physical proof that they can do the job, but it has to be said that hardly anybody else will be impressed. Sometimes this drive for volume can have its comical side. Thus a class of information science students were set an on-line exercise to discover what the Winter of 1989 was like. The searching was conducted on a full-text newspaper database – FT PROFILE. After about twenty minutes a very unhappy student put up a hand for help. The problem? Well, they had only found one article. The fact that the article gave all the details mattered not, something was driving them on to find more of the same!

On the whole people are quite aware of their information appetite so it makes a good deal of sense to ask them how many documents/pages etc. they would ideally like in response to their query. That way they can juggle the need for comprehensive information with the constraints placed upon them. More likely, there will be a preference for limited information that meets deadlines rather than complete information that does not. Peoples are subject to a whole array of communication forms – the information centre rarely has a majority stake in information provision, and this needs to be taken into account when assessing the information appetite for information centre-generated data.

Quality/authority

Assessments of the quality of information may be highly subjective, but, nevertheless, quality ranks very highly on the list of information priorities. The highly vocal, on-going debate about the quality of information on the Web is a testament to this. Quality concerns loom particularly large in the light of the information explosion that is currently being experienced. Quality determinants are obviously very important in reducing the information pile. Selection inevitably has to take place and far better that it is conducted along logical grounds than arbitrary ones. Not so long ago it was said that academics and researchers had the time, inclination and skill to take quality decisions themselves and that it was practitioners that really needed the help, but with the changes in academic contracts, increased workloads and increased student numbers, even academics need help.

Some fields and occupations require that particular attention be paid to the veracity of information – crime, business and science are cases in point. This quote from a leading crime correspondent: *there is a problem with inaccurate information and particularly in my field that could be very dangerous because we run into problems of libel and we run into problems of contempt. It is obviously less dangerous in other areas of reporting like say the environment or arts. Reporting crime if you get bogus information or inaccurate information about people's convictions or about crimes – then you are in trouble and I am wary of the Internet for that reason.* Scientists are another group who have stringent quality and accuracy requirements.

To select information on quality grounds you need a very good understanding of the information producers in the subject field and, of course, it can be a highly personal decision. There are though, a number of aids that can help, and which are employed by knowledgeable users all the time. The perceived authority of the sender or source is probably the principal aid. Take what someone said about the information giver: *one of the filters on what stuff you read is who sends it to you; the weight given to the information will depend on the source providing that information and more weight will be given to information provided by a source if that source has a high position in an organisation.* People are aware that certain organisations, because of their economic or political power, command particular authority or respect and, as a consequence, their publications or Web sites carry a lot of clout. This would be true of the Government, the European Union and some academic establishments, for instance. Perhaps as a consequence of people's concerns over the quality of the information on the Web, Government Web sites are particularly popular – in fact they are the most popular amongst journalists. Thus the science editor at *The Guardian* regularly consults sites such as The NASA Pathfinder mission, The American Association for the Advancement of Science, The Global Siesmology Unit, in pursuit of quality information. He unquestioningly accepts that the information from such bodies will be accurate and reliable (whether conveyed via the Internet, hard copy press release or any other means) and is prepared to incorporate it straight into his stories.

Some commercial organisations carry a lot of respect as a result of the quality of their work and excellent track record. Take the case of stockbrokers in the City of London. Every month they get dozens of voluminous, extremely well presented reports from analysts forecasting movements in the stock market and recommending stocks. No dealer or market maker could ever find the time to remove themselves from the computer screens to read them. Instead the majority of them are placed in the bin and just a few read, almost always including the one from James Capel. And why James Capel and not the others? Well, for many years they were voted the best research house in the City – here peer evaluation is the deciding factor in reducing the information load. But perceptions of authority can and do change and it is no longer James Capel that wins all the plaudits now, but some other stockbroker.

In nearly every academic discipline there is a pecking order of journals – the universal nature of the pecking order being dependent upon the level of consensus in the field. This is most obvious in science, where users can rank journals on impact or quality grounds, and the level of agreement amongst them would be exceedingly high. They can do this because they know – usually through the process of submitting manuscripts – that certain journals are harder to get an article published in than others: the cream rises to the surface. Readers recognise this: *If I read an article in Nature or The Journal of the British Medical Association then it is not an unreasonable assumption that the guy knows what he's talking about and that his colleagues believe he knows what he is talking about.* Nature appears to be everybody's first choice, regardless of scientific discipline or nationality. Therefore *Nature* can be very choosy. If they cannot get into *Nature* they go to the next one down the ladder – usually the most pre-eminent journal in their own discipline. More often than not they know what the quality of their research is and send the article to a journal that reflects that quality. Quality thus tiers down and users make use of this fact to ensure that if they only have time to read, say, five journals out of a possible fifty, they know precisely which ones they will read. Above all they would not want to miss the articles that made waves, got colleagues talking etc. This process has now been enshrined in the Government's Research Assessment Exercise, which measures the quality of university research. As part of this every participating Department has to enter the best four publications of each member of its staff. Refereed articles count the highest.

Some sources are so authoritative that they can set the political and news agenda, or make the lead story. Thus the BBC Radio 4's Today programme is widely recognised throughout the media and political worlds as being agenda setting – largely because of its flagship status and because important and authoritative people are drawn to its studios. Also articles from *Nature* or *The Lancet* frequently make the television or radio news, when a new piece of research is released. Articles in newspapers like the *Financial Times* and the *Wall Street Journal* can actually move financial markets and bring down economies. In one of its advertising campaigns the *Financial Times* played upon the crucial role it has in meeting the information needs of the business world – *no FT, no comment* was the advertising slogan.

Newspapers are invested with special authority by many people. It is not because people believe all they read in newspapers or necessarily trust everything that is in them, it is just that their wide and large readership – including lots of decision makers, means that what they say has a great impact. Obviously the corollary of all this is that some sources lack authority. Thus, for journalists, the authority of press releases is very suspect indeed. In fact, journalists are extremely concerned with authority. Much of the unsolicited material that comes to them looks suspiciously like propaganda, public relations or advertising: it is difficult to distinguish fact from hype. In consequence, a good deal of cross-checking is done. At *The Economist*, for instance, where none of the articles are signed – and as a result the reputation of the whole magazine is at stake, unchecked facts and unverified sources are simply not used. An advertisement for the journal once stated: *The Economist believes in collective responsibility. It commits its own reputation to every sentence it writes, good or bad.* Indeed, *Economist* journalists take the authority invested in them extremely seriously. Take the following story as an example: at one editorial board the following week's edition was being considered, and the conversation got around to an article about Mozambique. The question was, should the article appear the week before the forthcoming elections or during election week? One journalist argued that the article should appear the week before, because, that way, the powers that be in Mozambique would read it and that would stop them making the same mistake as they did the time before!

Authority can also come from having used a source successfully before – it is tried and trusted. Amongst practitioners in particular there is a strong preference for the known, established, and trusted information source over the new and untried source. Sometimes this can lead to problems, with individuals reluctant to move on to a new source or even an updated edition of the original one. New sources are always suspect on grounds of their authority. Information professionals surely have a role here in helping to'roll out' new products.

Other ways of establishing quality are through book/CD reviews and citation analysis. Book reviews have long been the librarian's favoured tool, but their value is limited by their (lack of) currency and by the fact that only a few books are ever reviewed. New information services that link book reviews with bibliographic records, like TES-Bookfind, are undoubtedly an assistance here. Most CD Web sites also link products to reviews. Citation analysis can help in the identification of authoritative journal articles – it can help with books and reports too. From such services as Social Citation Index, highly cited documents can easily be identified – offering up probably the best example of direct peer evaluation that there is.

Computerised information systems pose problems when it comes to authority. Firstly, their sheer size and numerous access points mean that searches are frequently characterised by the large number of irrelevant documents that they produce – natural language computerised databases are particularly good at emptying the barrel. This has made a number of users – like politicians and lawyers – fight shy of searching them. There is another side to this. Computerised data of the kind supplied by online hosts, like Dialog and FT Profile, come stripped of the conventional authority markers, like typeface, logo, cover etc. The data all looks the same. This was thought to be the problem with the Web too, but this information mammoth appears to have changed our perceptions of what constitutes authority. The fact that the Web comes with no track whatsoever, has given birth to a whole raft of new information sources – Amazon.com, for instance, means that the whole notion of authority is surely up for grabs.

In many respects the mass production of information WWW style is more like a feature of an industrial society than an information society because of the way in which quality and individuality has been sacrificed for the great god production. The Web takes little cognisance of the fact that, for instance, financial, military, and medical information domains are definitely built upon quality information. The digital mobile phone is quite different. Quality control will become a major concern for mobile information services because their users will pay for quality, not for the information itself.

There is a very important role here for the information professional in providing quality assessments, especially in the construction of information-filtering mechanisms that take account of quality criteria. Quite clearly Web search engines and their relevance-ranking methods are not up to that job.

Date/currency

Two closely related questions have to be asked regarding this information needs characteristic: firstly, how far back in·time is information required; and secondly, how up-to-date does the information need to be? The first is largely dependent upon the shelf-life of information in the field. There are huge differences. Thus, in science and some of the applied social sciences, citation studies show that information has a relatively short life: less than five years in many cases, and probably less than two years in the case of computing. Obsolescence occurs as a result of change: new discoveries, new equipment, computerisation, political and economic factors and legislation can render valueless – even dangerous, what we know and do. For instance, consider the value today of a book published on central heating systems for the home in the 1980s – books that can still be found in some public libraries. The relative prices of fuels have changed; much of the equipment featured would be obsolete, and new energy saving features would not be mentioned. News and technical information are probably most subject to obsolescence.

In the case of the humanities the very opposite can be true: that is information actually gains value with age. Something written by Hitler during the Second World War would be valued for its age – it would be a source document. By its very nature it cannot be superseded. Even in the sciences not all information ages rapidly, the theory and fundamentals of many subjects are fairly constant and, as a result, long-established (but revised) textbooks and manuals are still well-thumbed. Medicine often needs long-term retrospective information in considering the development of a disease. People often intuitively know what the obsolescence factor is in their field and should be asked for this information. If they cannot remember their computer logs will probably reveal the truth.

It is not just shelf life of the information that determines the date range required – the amount of time that a person has available to read and digest information also comes into it. Date of origin is frequently used as a means of selection – sometimes, as a substitute for quality. It is a useful cut-off point for a search that produces a lot of documents. That is why so many on-line systems order their output in reverse chronological order. The underlying belief being that the most current information is the most important information – something which Web search engines generally fail to recognise.

Currency is only one aspect of the date range requirement, but the pressing need to always have the very latest information puts it very much in the spotlight. No matter how far back in time individuals search for information they are always likely to require the most up-to-date information as well. Everybody has to keep up-to-date and – by definition – the new captures the most interest. People differ in their perception of what constitutes current information, although the Web has raised everybody's expectations. A marketmaker in a leading stockbroking firm would probably consider the last few minutes' information to be current, but for the historian the definition of current might well extend to a year or more. Every one works with a mix of new and old information: even stockbrokers, preoccupied as they are with the telephones and real-time wire services, need to place data into a context.

Obviously, for information to retain its currency it must be distributed quickly – something which is taken up more fully in the next section. Some information channels are more conducive to the rapid transmission of information than others: hence the tremendous popularity of e-mail, the mobile telephone and fax machine. Traditional information systems have never been geared to providing access to really current information – typically abstracting services still serve up information that is three to six-months old, and claim they are providing a current awareness function! Hence their unpopularity with practitioners, for whom currency of data is everything. (Academics, whose currency requirements are less stringent, exhibit a tolerance towards abstracting services). Fortunately, on-line technology and the Internet are enabling information professionals to get much closer to what people regard as acceptably current information. For instance, FT Profile provides same day access to the full text of some newspaper articles. Real-time services, like those provided by the Press Association (PA) and Reuters, are now also the domain of information professionals.

As previously noted the Internet is doing much to raise the currency performance, but too often it flatters to deceive. Sites are sometimes not even as up-to-date as their hard-copy equivalents. Currency is not always as obvious: the 'date stamp' is not as prominent, and sometimes missing all together. It is far more prominent in hard-copy services.

The provision of current information is the hallmark of a good information system – and for many people it is a performance indicator by which they measure the efficiency of the library or information system. That is why on-line systems, rather than CD-ROMs, are such an invaluable asset and marketing tool for information professionals.

Information professionals have long understood this characteristic of need – and the chronological arrangement of date is a well-established practice. Of course, information units and systems themselves have a need to weed, discard and archive information, because of the cost and space involved in storing information. This is often done using date criteria. Thus at *The Economist* they really only keep the current year's information: this represents a trade-off between use and the cost of storing data.

However, where information professionals often have got it wrong is in holding on to information long after it has become deceased (the collector syndrome), and in failing to understand the complex relationship between occupation/job role and currency requirements. Thus just because journalists deal with news as it is breaking does not mean that they do not need archival information. In fact they do – to put the breaking news into some kind of context.

Speed of delivery

Speed of delivery is all about getting information to people fast – as fast as the need for it. Obviously information should not go 'off' in transit or transmission. Thus news has a very short shelf life and should, say, an abstracting service provide abstracts of news items months late as sometimes is the case (*British Humanities Index* for instance) then its value as a publicist of news information is severely circumscribed. Traditional information services generally respond relatively slowly and that must account for their low take-up by practitioners in particular. It was not so long ago that The British Library Document Supply Centre's inter-library loan performance of 5-7 days from query to receipt of document was – and still is by some – being trumpeted as a success story. And it can still take academic libraries three months to order a new book and put it on the shelf. However, full-text on-line services, electronic document delivery, the fax and, most recently, the Internet have all come to the aid of the information centre to make for – in theory, anyway – a much more responsive service. Many information units still trundle along in the traditional leisurely fashion – ignoring the huge changes that have occurred around them, making them look almost prehistoric by comparison. Thus Amazon.com's ability to get a book to a user within the week has shone the spotlight on the performance of most libraries in getting books to their customers. Even people that do not need information that quickly are impressed by rapid response – after all, it is another performance measure. It is synonymous with efficiency.

Speed of delivery in its turn has an affect on currency, for the faster people can get information, the more current it is and that drives up their currency expectations, with people wanting ever more current data. Furthermore, with increased speeds of delivery, thanks to information technology, a more instant response is demanded of everyone: knee-jerk reactions become the norm. Take the case of the stockbroker. Twenty-five years ago human messengers would bring price information from the Stock Exchange twice a day and maybe this information would arrive twenty minutes late. On arrival of the prices a frenetic period of activity would begin. This would subside after a while and then the stockbrokers would prepare themselves (perhaps by reading) for the next price announcements that came much later in the day. Now, however, thanks to real-time on-line systems, they watch the prices change on the screen in front of them, seconds after they have been posted. This goes on all day long, there is no relief or quiet time – they watch the screens all the time. Today's working environments are characterised by the urgency and immediacy with which tasks have to be done and in such an environment it is not surprising that rapid information delivery is highly prized – almost above everything else. In newspapers, for instance, if information cannot be obtained within half an hour or so it will simply not be used. Hence, the enormous popularity of the telephone, e-mail and fax in today's offices.

Speed, speed and more speed appear to be what most people want – and this applies as much to information as it does to transport. In cognisance of this fact Web designers and computer manufacturers continue to see the reduction of response times as their main goal. Probably, it is with regard to information delivery times that the Internet has had the greatest impact. The ability to access information from the far-reaches of the world, at anytime of the day, in a matter of minutes, if not seconds must be regarded as one of the information wonders of the world. Also the live broadcast qualities of the Web have taken information delivery into a new and exciting league. Because of this it is highly likely that news will increasingly migrate from hard-copy newspapers to newspaper web sites, possibly reducing newspapers to features magazines.

In a news item in *The Independent*, describing the benefits of fax for information retrieval, the obviously smitten author notes that *At the touch of the button, anyone with a facsimile machine and a touch-tone telephone can ring the service and have information sent over immediately by fax.* He ends with the question, *Whither the first-class post when the home facsimile comes of age?* (MacRae, 1993). He could have been asking that question of traditional libraries, too.

Place

Despite talk of the global society, the place or country of origin of information matters to some people. This is recognised by such search engines as Yahoo, which offers the opportunity to restrict a search by country. It is not information about a country that is of concern, for that is a subject concern. Of course, there is some linkage, for if you wished to study, say the politics of Cyprus, then you would be well advised to examine the publications emanating from that island. Whether place matters or not depends largely on three things: (1) subject; (2) language proficiency; and, (3) whether the user is a practitioner or academic.

Subject

The subject matter of some fields is truly international and its geographical origins are largely secondary. Science is a case in point. If someone is studying cancer or salmonella poisoning they are likely to be interested in research emanating from anywhere in the world. This is shown to best effect in scientific journal publishing, where no matter what the geographic origin of the publisher, the authorship is likely to be international – and probably so too is the publisher. However, even in science, users will place a higher priority on the literature of some countries than others. Some countries are held in higher regard, because of the quality and size of their research, and others are simply not rated at all, because of the poverty of theirs. In this regard the literature of the USA is universally held in high esteem and the literature of the Third World generally ignored. In defence, scientists would point out that if, say, someone from Indonesia had something really worthwhile to say they would say it in a Western journal, for the recognition and prestige it would bring them. It is often through international conferences that scientists (qualitatively) sample the non-western literature. The fact that largely one language – English – is used for international communication of major results in science obviously helps too.

In the social sciences things can be very different. The lack of universally accepted methodologies and definitions, and uniquely national social institutions (like the UK's National Health Service for instance) tends to mean information gathering is much more parochial. Also, English is not the unifying force that it is in science. But it is so for some subjects in the social sciences – economics and psychology, for instance, have broad international horizons. Indeed, economics/business have become so international in the light of the removal of trade barriers, the freeing up of financial markets and the dropping of exchange controls, that national economic policies, like interest rates, are determined by external factors, like a drop in the international market for bonds, and not only by national or domestic ones. However, in subjects like law and social welfare, communication is country-bound, although the European Union is increasingly drawing even law out of its traditional insularity. In the case of social welfare the concerns are more local – at the regional rather than national level. In the cases of some social science and humanities subjects – history and geography come most immediately to mind – countries are the subjects of study and, as a result, place of origin is of special importance to them. Taking place of publication to its logical extreme (i.e. the immediate work environment), it has been found that higher weight is given to information produced by the host organisation – it is, of course, immediately relevant and directly touches upon the individual. Civil servants show a general preference for in-house information sources that are controlled by them.

Practitioner/academic divide

Academics, because they tend to be more interested in ideas – and even in the social sciences theories travel well (viz. Marxism and Feminism), and comparative approaches, adopt a more international approach to information gathering than practitioners. Practitioners and consumers probably obtain most of their foreign information second-hand from the national news services. It is said that, because of global telecommunications, the world is getting smaller (hence the term the Global Village) and it might be expected that people will – not necessarily knowingly – feed off a more international diet of information in the future. The growth of satellite television, the arrival of the Internet and the fact that some of the most heavily watched television programmes in the UK are American or Australian, is cited in support of this view. Citation studies have shown that international communication is not a two-way or reciprocal process. Thus the US literature, because of its sheer size, research muscle, and better system for marketing and distributing information, has a significant impact on most countries. However, it has also been noted that Americans are quite self-sufficient in their use of information and take only an occasional interest in the literatures or, even affairs, of other countries. When the Ro Ro Ferry sank in the Baltic in September 1994, taking with it the lives of 900 people, the British newspapers gave it continuous and often front-page treatment, despite the fact that barely a handful of British people were involved. In the US press it merited a mere paragraph.

Language proficiency

Linguistic ability obviously helps determine whether information from foreign countries is consumed. There are still the language barriers in place that were referred to so often in the professional literature of the Sixties. Research points to the fact that, even when people can read foreign literature, they are not highly motivated to do so. Mindful of this, the European Union publishes all its significant papers in all the languages of the Community. The Web is helping overcome language barriers in two main ways. Firstly, it is encouraging people of all languages to disseminate information in English to obtain the largest audience. Well over 80% of Web sites are in English. Secondly, a number of search engines provide a translating facility.

Again, the Web has had a major impact on this area of need. The impact is not a straightforward one though. By making it much easier to get hold of information from any country on earth it is promoting the use of 'foreign' material. However, because the vast majority of information on the Web is from the US, use is even more concentrated.

Processing and packaging

These two characteristics of need are closely related and overlapping and are best treated together.

Processing refers to the different ways that the same ideas and research can be represented. Thus for the same topic a researcher might want raw data with as little manipulation and interpretation as possible (unprocessed data), whereas a practitioner or consumer might want the bare bones of data, with really only the significance of the data being spelt out (highly processed data). In fact, a single scientific discovery, social survey, government inquiry can be processed for a whole range of audiences and purposes and this happens all the time. Take a piece of research undertaken on the effect of increased lighting on crime in a housing estate in East London. The work was originally published as a Home Office research report. As a research report it was typically densely and closely argued, full of data, descriptions of research methods and statistical appendices, and really only accessible to other researchers. However, the topic itself was of interest to a much wider audience. Consequently it was then condensed and fashioned for an article in a professional journal and, after that, it was picked up by the newspapers and finally featured as a one minute item on the local television news. At every stage in this chain detail was removed, interpretation featured more strongly and the information content was reduced. In this case, and in most cases, condensation and simplification took place at each level of processing, resulting in a reduction in the quantity of information. Processing usually involves a reduction in the quantity of information – and hence its chief attraction, but it need not do so, for condensation and simplification are not the same things.

The kind of processing observed above largely involves popularisation. There are other specialist forms – interpretations, reviews, abstracts, and executive summaries. Web pages may also be seen to be a form of processing and popularisation. In that respect they have more in common with television and tabloid newspapers. There is alleged to be great skill involved in page design – and such skill commands a lot of money. The great concern shown over computer interfaces is as much a concern about processing as anything else. This characteristic of need is one that commands the greatest respect by Web designers – almost to the point of distraction it should be said.

Other than the Web, people come into contact with heavily processed information when they read the newspaper, listen to the radio or watch TV. Specialist correspondents spend a good deal of their time simplifying, popularising and explaining government reports, research studies and major surveys – and they are generally very good at this, making all kinds of difficult topics accessible to the uninitiated. It is quite likely that television reports are so highly processed that they probably pass through the system without ever being absorbed by the brain. So, maybe the process can be taken too far?

Of the specialist forms of processing the one very dear to the information professionals' heart is the abstract. However, with perhaps the exception of scientists and academics – many of whom provide the abstracts – they are not especially popular amongst users. This is probably because, in many cases, abstracting results in too much loss of information. Unfortunately, in this commercially sensitive information world – which rates above all else production numbers, the short pithy indicative (but uninformative) abstract seems to be taking hold. The abstracts that TEXTLINE used to provide before they moved over to a largely full-text system were probably ideal – and users actually preferred them to the full text. They were highly factual, often fusing two or more related news items together, and in some cases, resembled the original so much that copyright was close to being infringed. Hence their demise. Abstracts are not always helpful unless one subscribes to academic journals or has access to a large public or academic library.

Book reviews are another form of processing and if a report in the *Evening Standard* is anything to go by they – together with the 'blurbs' – are frequently the only part of a book that is ever read. The value of book reviews is enhanced by their attachment to bibliographic entries on book databases.

Senior management and busy professionals generally require highly processed information. With attention spans measured in a few minutes, the one-side A4 sheet listing bullet points, is the preferred document form.

Packaging in this context means the external presentation or physical form of the information – the form in which it is stored and communicated. The relationship between processing and packaging is a very close one, because certain information packages are designed for the storage and dissemination of specific levels of processed data. Thus dissertations and theses are packages that convey a good deal of data and detail. So do research reports and statistical series. Almost inevitably then, there is a limited audience for these information packages. Conversely, the Internet, newspapers, television and leaflets – all purveyors of highly processed information have vast and popular audiences. Of course, it is not always as simple as that, for theses have abstracts and broad sheet newspapers have their heavy articles, and it is almost impossible to typecast books.

However, it is not the level of processing alone that attracts users to various forms of information package. There is a lot more to it than that, for as we have seen already some packages are more current than others (the Web, news-wires); some are far more exclusive (oral sources); some demand much less of the individual in digesting their messages (television); some have much greater status and appeal (mobile phones); others are very accessible (newspapers); and some are just plainly more familiar (books). The personality of the individual comes into it too – there are those who are more comfortable with oral sources, or the mobile phone, for instance. Thus a person's preference for a certain package is likely to be a result of an amalgamation of factors. Because packages are the physical embodiment of information it is not surprising that users require that their information should be presented to them in a certain package – often to the exclusion of others. Thus scientists have a love affair with journals, students cannot get enough of the Web, newspaper cuttings similarly smite journalists, and community workers revel in grey literature. Often it is the case that people prefer the forms in which they regularly communicate. This is hardly surprising, but it is something that can lead to tunnel vision as the media correspondent of the *Evening Standard* points out: *We* [journalists] *do not know enough about the world. we rely too much on other newspapers* [for information]... (Glover, 1994).

Information professionals are very well acquainted with this characteristic of need; indeed, they are probably guilty of giving it too much prominence. After all, they do spend a good deal of their time organising and storing these packages – hard-copy and digital. All too often it is a package and not the information that is given in answer to a question. They are guilty of showing bias towards some packages. Thus the traditional library is full of books and journals. Newspapers, leaflets, videos, unpublished information and personal contacts are generally neglected, even when they would appear to be more appropriate in dealing with the enquiry. Some information professionals feel it is more worthy and productive to catalogue a book rather than a pamphlet or keeping a contact register up-to-date.

And, as a result, they neglect these sources. In the case of the academic librarian it could be a case of responding to the wishes of their users, who might have a preference for authoritative sources – sources which in turn can be cited as acceptable evidence (e.g. Einstein *wrote* ranks ahead of Einstein *said*). Personal contacts may be useful for background information. For instance, about pitfalls to be avoided, or information about work in progress.

Because of their practical concerns with form (storage etc.), information professionals tend to build information systems for certain publication forms – and so fragment and complicate the search for information. Thus the OPACs in most of our college libraries provide access only to books (something students are often totally unaware of). The periodicals – arguably a far more suitable and expensive resource are largely left to a scattered and mismatched set of abstracting/indexing services. The multimedia capabilities of the Web have made everybody re-think the ghettoisation of information packages. Perhaps, the Web is becoming a ghetto, too?

Overview

Information system designers and managers should take note of all needs characteristics, but some characteristics are deserving of extra attention. Especially:

(1)　the immediacy and urgency of need (the speed of delivery) – response times are everything in this rapid-response world;

(2) the uncertainty of need in a world of seemingly constant change – systems should allow for economic and purposeful browsing and take a lead from modern bookshops that seem to understand the need to rummage;

(3) the highly personal nature of need – so providing filtering and targeting mechanisms to make information more amenable to the individual;

(4) the authority/quality requirements that are becoming ever more important in the light of the information flood unleashed by the Internet.

The characteristics of information need have been comprehensively dealt with, but that is not to say that using the recommended form of analysis is a long and laborious task. It is the understanding that takes the time. Once the form of analysis is mastered, then the various sections outlined here shrink into a headings check list. The time taken to undertake an assessment depends on the task that is being considered. If it is simply a case of running an on-line search for someone, then 10 minutes is the time being talked about – not an inordinate amount of time considering the importance of the task and the cost involved. In the case of setting up an SDI service or evaluating an information system the questioning will be somewhat more painstaking, but then this task has to be undertaken less often. The act of delegation deserves due care and attention. Delegation is all about trust and would you trust someone who thought they could understand you in a matter of seconds?

The routine collection and analysis of information needs data should be a central management activity. The successful management of change means having good quality monitoring data that can be fed into decision-making. Information needs assessments should not be seen as one-off exercises. Unless you are conducting them at least twice a year you are not undertaking them regularly enough.

5. Factors Involved in the Meeting of Information Needs

Whether or not someone sets about gathering and using information in response to a problem that requires additional information depends on a mixture of factors – some of which we have touched on already. The main ones that we will briefly deal with here are:

- the kind of job the person does;
- the country/culture from which they come from;
- the personality of the individual and their information threshold;
- their level of information awareness/training;
- the gender of the person;
- the age of the person;
- time availability;
- access
- resources/costs;
- information overload.

Job/occupation

The nature of the job must have a huge influence on information-seeking. It is not just the case that some jobs are more information demanding than others – journalism is an example of a very information-hungry profession. There is also the fact that the penalties that result from acting in the absence of information are greater for certain jobs and tasks than others. Thus in research science, which has a very open peer-evaluated information system, it is somewhat easier to spot that someone has not kept up-to-date. In fields like medicine the consequences of acting without the benefit of the best information can indeed be grave, and in law and the City it could be incredibly costly. It is not surprising that in these fields you see the most sophisticated and up-to-date information systems. Students are an interesting case. Students' information needs are dictated to them by their lecturers – and to make sure their information needs can be met, lecturers give them lists of readings and web sites. A more tightly regulated information environment you could not get – and one which you would think would be a guarantee of certain success. Despite being told that the more reading they do the better will be their grade, students frequently fail to read. Plainly, they have made a trade-off between effort and risk. The trade-off is reasonably well executed because most pass. However, if a student is asked to read in order to give a seminar presentation, they will – the penalties for ignorance now far outweigh the expenditure of effort involved.

There are other work-related factors that come into play: experience in the job, seniority, whether it is a solitary or team-based occupation. The more experienced a person, the more knowledge they will have picked up as a result and the less need they will have to go chasing it. They are also more likely to have a good informal communication network to help them find information when they need it. Seniority can be a related issue, but need not be so. The more senior the person, the better their access to information – information normally comes into an organisation from the top, and the better resources they are likely to command. Also the more senior the person the more likely they are to delegate: pressures on executive time and the low status associated with (formal) information-seeking being the reasons. People who work in teams have greater opportunities to share information, especially orally.

Country/culture

Attributing information behavioural patterns to cultural factors is somewhat more contentious, and the evidence is rather more anecdotal in nature. Just as some people are undoubtedly more organised, motivated etc. than others (a point taken up further in the personality section), the same too can be said about nations or cultures. A good example of this was given on the BBC TV's Business Breakfast programme. The supervisor of a computer telephone help-line, based in Milton Keynes, but servicing the whole of Europe, was asked whether the different European nations had different problems and asked different questions. She said they did, and mentioned the Germans as an example. Apparently the Germans always ask very specific questions, after having studied the manual in some detail beforehand. In comparison, the British never read their manuals and, as a result, their questions were broad and unfocussed. Probably the best known national trait – and this is relatively well documented, is the insular nature of the information-seeking of US academics. Citation studies have shown, time and time again, that Americans hardly ever use the literature of other countries – even when the topic being studied is located in these other countries.

Personality

Patently some people possess psychological characteristics that are beneficial to information-seeking and gathering – they maybe more organised or more motivated, for instance. Psychological factors may exert the greatest influence on information-seeking. The following factors are probably the most influential.

- **Persistence**. The willingness to continue the hunt for information over a (reasonable) period of time. To try again with a new approach or strategy when initial forays have proved unsuccessful or unrewarding.

- **Thoroughness**. The willingness to search deeply, but not necessarily over time, and to leave no stone unturned. To be painstaking when searching for or evaluating information.

- **Orderliness.** Being orderly in regard to both the retrieval and storage of information. The quality of being systematic: keeping records, preparing searches, organising bookmarks, and possessing systematic filing systems.

- **Motivation.** The commitment to the job, the task or the client. Obviously, motivation can be influenced by the nature of the job, what you are paid and the people that you work with. If you feel jaundiced with the job, kicking your heels after many years in an unfulfilling job, no matter what your own personal disposition is, you are likely to be de-motivated. Persistence and thoroughness come with motivation.

- **Receptiveness.** The willingness to accept information from others: friends, colleagues or information officers. This is probably a key determinant in whether the information search is delegated or not. There is also a possible link with gender here – it has been argued that women are more receptive than men are, a link taken up further a little later.

Of course fundamental personality traits are involved here: introversion/extroversion, neuroticism/stability, for instance, and inertia plays a fundamental role in the case of persistence and thoroughness. In many respects there is little that information professionals can do about the possession or non-possession of these influential characteristics, though training can obviously help in regard to the first three characteristics, and management certainly has a role to play when it comes to motivation.

Information threshold is the ability to take on-board information. Capacity and the rate of absorption may limit this ability. It many respects this all comes down to a person's intelligence: it has little to do with personality. The brighter the person the more they absorb and the faster they can absorb it. Writers shy away from the discussion of intelligence, because of its elitist connotations, but no one could deny that intelligence is a major determinant in information-seeking behaviour. But this is patently not true of the ownership of communication channels – satellite television or mobile phones, for example.

Awareness/training

You can only use what you know about and what you are experienced or trained in using. In a world mushrooming with new technologically advanced information sources and systems this is always going to be a problem. While end-user skills have undoubtedly come on in recent years most still demonstrate a woeful knowledge of: (a) what is out there – the unfathomable and bottomless Web has provided them with cover for their ignorance; (b) how to search the systems/databases they actually find. Indeed, this is why users are quite happy to delegate the search to an information professional. In fact they often prefer to do this rather than be trained themselves. Research has often shown that information professionals – despite their relatively low numbers, come out as the biggest, most regular, expert users of all kinds of information systems. Plainly expertise and training are factors here.

Gender

There is increasing evidence to suggest that women approach information-seeking rather differently than men. Deborah Tannen (1991) in a substantial *Guardian* article, which explored the different ways that women and men communicate with each other, touched upon many issues relevant to information-seeking behaviour. In particular, she noted how important sharing information is to women and how it helped to cement social relationships. The withholding of information deprived relationships of their closeness or intimacy. For men the withholding of information meant that they could hold tight the reins of power or protect the women from information they considered not to be in their best interest. Tannen also pointed to men's unwillingness to ask questions of others. She tells the story of a couple driving to a friends for dinner. They get lost and the woman asks the man to stop and ask a passer-by for guidance. He refuses preferring to find the way without help. He persists in this manner until they are hopelessly lost. For Tannen the man does not ask for directions because that would be an admission of failure, whereas, for the women, asking for information has no such connotations. Indeed, the act of communication and sharing information was a pleasurable one. In another *Guardian* article Deborah Jackson (1993) examined the role of memory in a gender context. She pointed out that *memory is a selective thing... and that women's recollections of certain personal events are more vivid, if not more accurate, than those of men were.* In a marriage women are the family archivists and historians, remembering birthdays, anniversaries etc. Men are assigned to remember information related to household maintenance.

Studies have also found a link between gender and information system use. Men tend to be the early leaders. Also women seem to experience more problems when online, although it is just possible that they are more honest then men.

Age

Of course, age often brings with it seniority and experience. Though this seems not to be so much so with Internet-related work. Age makes some people less mobile and less adventurous – possibly, because of physical disability. In information terms this may manifest itself in using only what is close to hand – making fewer visits to libraries as a result. Age may also de-motivate the person, making them less likely to want to meet their needs. Age does appear to be a factor in the non-use of information technology but not quite in the way you might suspect. Amongst journalists for instance the heaviest Internet users are the middle-aged. These people have had the benefits of searching online hosts and have the resources and time to search the Web. This is a discernible drop in use over 55 but this could change as technologically literate graduates start filtering through the age bands.

Time

A useful distinction can be made between the time people have available for searching and digesting information, and the time limit within which information has to be gathered and used. Often this is the same thing, but sometimes it is not. Thus in theory, journalists have as much time in the day as academics, but unlike academics, their information-seeking is limited by – and presses up against – the daily deadlines of the newspaper.

A lack of time is what commonly prevents most people from meeting their information needs, even those who are motivated to do so. Most people today work in a hothouse environment where they are increasingly asked to do more in the same amount of time. Frequent changes and interruptions during the working day compound the problem. Because people are working harder, faster and undertaking a wider range of activities than ever before, there is just not the time to obtain the necessary information. Even when computerised systems come to people's aid, the gain is soon lost, because the competition also adopts the same solutions. Back to square one? Not quite, everything now moves that much faster. There is seldom time to spend any time on one activity or topic. This encourages knee-jerk reactions rather than considered ones. In such environments, the only information systems or channels that will be used are those which respond fast and provide information that can be consumed quickly (the ubiquitous information bite). Information has to be short, to the point and to be obtained and digested in the time allotted for that task.

Never underestimate how little time people have available for information acquisition and digestion. In the words of one social worker: *the sheer pressures of the day frequently mean the reading of books or journals, indeed reading itself, are pushed aside.* Nor should we neglect the growing ranks of the retired and the unemployed. For all these people, in theory anyway, a lack of time is not the main problem – too much time may be.

Access

If there are no information sources or systems available or immediately to hand then it is highly unlikely that people will be able to meet their information needs or engage in information-seeking behaviour. There are two things to consider: whether in fact a source/system is available at all and – if it is – how far away is it. Obviously, if it is a long way off, then you might as well not have it in the first place. Thanks to electronic and computerised means of communication and retrieval, geographical distances have been shrunk and, indeed, now have no significance at all. And while the only way of remaining instantly informed on a whole range of topics fifty years ago was to live next to the British Museum or the Bodleian Library, this no longer holds. It is frequently quicker to search Dialog in California than go up a floor to the library. So the information resource has come closer – very close if you have a networked PC on your desk, that provides access to the Internet and commercial on-line services. But it is all relative. Whereas once accessibility was measured in miles it is now measured in metres, if not centimetres. It is not unusual for a user to prefer an information system just because it is on their PC rather than on a dedicated terminal just a metre away. That was certainly the case at *The Guardian* where the absence of desk-top access to the Internet was a major factor in that resource's under use. Laptop computers and mobile phones take access into a new league – you don't even have to be at your desk to obtain the information you need.

Information use and proximity go hand-in-glove, as *The Guardian* Library discovered when they were relocated within the Farringdon Road building. Previously, they had been situated close to Home news reporters – their biggest users. The Sports department was on another floor and never used them – it was thought that this was because they simply did not need the library as their field was very narrow and they were all enthusiasts (remembering all they needed to know). However, the library moved to the floor on which Sport was located, and since then they have become one of their biggest users. Being able to get information more easily and quickly was obviously a major factor here, but we must not neglect the fact that seeing the information resource must stimulate the information appetite or jog the mind. People will usually use what is easiest and what is closest to hand, and not what is necessarily best or most appropriate. They will take the path of least resistance, providing they have a choice.

It is for reasons of ease of access that people build up office collections, have telephones and computers on their desks, and mobiles in their pockets. The idea of immediate access, even if not fully realised in practice, is a very powerful one. And it is the need for immediate access that will drive the move towards using mobile phones as information retrieval platforms.

In the electronic age concerns over distance have been replaced by concerns over time – the time it takes to access the system/source (this is where the constraints of time and access merge). The slow response rates sometimes associated with the Internet have forced many people in the UK to shift their information-seeking to the morning, when the Americans – the system's biggest users are asleep. Bandwidths, like search engines, have become party talk.

There is another aspect to access: that is gaining access to the system once you have established physical contact with it. In addition to the difficulties encountered in coming to grips with the search interfaces – and allegedly user-friendly menu-driven services can create as many difficulties as command-driven ones – there is the problem of choosing the right terms with which to interrogate the system, and grappling with soft subject vocabularies. However, even if people are confronted by external and internal access problems they will find a way to overcome them. If the will is there and the drive for information sufficiently strong, users will conquer unfriendly search interfaces, keep trying to go on-line when they get "password in use" messages, walk a long way to find them, and then stand in queues when they get there. MPs' Research Assistants at the House of Commons were subject to all this and yet they still searched the systems with some alacrity (Nicholas *et al.*, 1990).

What happens when the person does not have access to a source or system. And here we are not simply talking about an inability to pay for it – that aspect is taken up in the next section. It could be a case of self-denial: feeling uncomfortable about approaching an individual because of their importance, lack of assertiveness, or feeling humbled by an impressive information system. Maybe also, the money is there, but the information culture is not – there is an aversion to spending money on information. Thus Social Service Departments went without libraries and information systems, despite having budgets – admittedly tight ones – stretching into millions of pounds. Putting new field social workers on the streets was always a higher priority than providing the existing ones with facilities for improving their access to information. So even if there was £50,000 to spare it would not be spent on information facilities, though political and economic pressures are rapidly changing the culture. But undoubtedly some cultures will not change for there are those 'managerial cultures,' which try to prevent information reaching subordinates.

Resources/costs

Not unconnected with access is the financial cost associated with acquiring information. Information systems and channels of communication are generally expensive, therefore they are likely to be found in the hands of the better-off. Plainly the Internet has brought these costs down – much to the chagrin of the commercial online hosts, but there are nevertheless considerable costs in their use (computer, printer, modem, telephone line and rental charges). The Government amongst others is especially worried about this in regard to the general public (and small businesses). The fear is that this will lead to sections of the public being socially excluded. Public libraries have been hit particularly hard. If they are to remain major players in information provision they will have to re-tool; replacing hard-copy encyclopaedias with CD-ROM ones, newspaper runs with a subscription to FT Profile and community files with Web sites. Despite Government funding to help get public libraries connected to the Internet, success in this enterprise is far from assured. Given the heterogeneous nature of public library clientele, they would probably need to retain hard-copy forms for many years to come. When the phrase 'information system' was synonymous with books, a few periodicals and a library, then the playing field was reasonably level – but not now.

In fields where information can be demonstrated to have a direct and immediate financial return – in stockbroking for instance – individuals will be very well provided for. After all, if millions of

pounds can be gained by the possession of information seconds ahead of the competitors, then why
worry about the thousands of pounds paid out on
information systems. It is nothing more than a
sound investment – and plainly seen as such. It is
not surprising that most of the big information in-
novations sprang from the financial field – full-text,
real-time systems for instance. In other fields – just
as worthy – the trade off is not as obvious. Information might have a social rather than economic
worth and as a result the financial priorities go elsewhere. Local government and the social services
are cases in point. In other fields not so financially
well-endowed large amounts of money are nevertheless spent on information systems, because they
have a strong information culture – Science is a
case in point. There is another culture – and one
encountered by anyone who has worked in the
public sector – and that is one in which the expectation is that information should be for free. In such
a culture it is almost a matter of principle that
money should not be spent on information. The
Internet has a culture a little bit like that. But you
first have to spend money to enter that culture.

Overload

In today's high-tech environment the information
bombardment rate can be truly phenomenal – there
is rarely time to catch one's breath. An article in
The Independent described what it was like for one
information-beleaguered City worker: *I come into
the office in the morning and there are reams of fax
paper from all over the world. I go to my answering*

machine to pick up my calls, and then I turn to my computer and find 72 messages in my electronic mail. It's an information explosion.(Williams 1993). The City worker forgot to mention the mail, the internal memos and the incessant round of meetings. It is not just in the practitioner environment that people are feeling the pressure, even in the backwater of academia it is claimed that *Teachers and students are drowning under a huge mass of information. Because of the sheer weight of information people are spending more time chasing it than absorbing it: people are spending 80 per cent of their time finding information, 10 per cent putting it in order and only 5 per cent of their time making decisions.* (Watts, 1994). Information can thus be a need and an obstacle to meeting that need. To protect themselves from the information tidal wave, people do a number of things. Senior managers insist that all written communication should fit on one-side of an A4 sheet (indeed, the further up the management scale the less the desire/need for detail); politicians employ researchers to filter their data for them; journalists do not 'switch' the Internet on; and social workers commonly turn their faces away from the published literature (relying on word of mouth instead).

Much has already been made of the sheer range of information channels people have today. Each new channel of information or information storage medium that comes along adds to the load. None seem to be supplanting earlier forms, indeed, the new ones actually appear to energise the old ones. Books were going to lose out to computers/video/television, but each piece of computer software comes with its manual; videos and television programmes generate big publishing opportunities, and a book shop (Amazon.com) was initially the success story of the Internet. It is hard to believe that forty years ago there really was no video, computer, e-mail, fax and mobile phone. More information is being beamed more quickly from more platforms at the individual. People are overdosing on information. Information gets in the way of finding information. Yet peoples' time to digest the information flow has been considerably reduced by so-called office efficiency drives and a generally faster pace to life. With more information coming out and less time to digest it the risk is that people are progressively seeing/using proportionally less and less information – much more information is passing them by. This is the ironic response of one member of the so-called Information Society; *there is too much information out there to feel well informed*. With the technological march still to gather full pace – digital interactive TV, Web TV and mobile/web phones have yet to impact, overload is likely to get worse.

For many people the Internet is synonymous with overload, and of the Internet facilities it is e-mail that causes the real fears. Fear of receiving junk e-mail in large quantities represented the most widespread reason why journalists fight shy of e-mail. *I get enough crap coming through the post without having to clear out my [e-mail] message queue every day* and, similarly, *The problem with e-mail is that there is no screening process – the crap comes straight in and I have to deal with it.*

There is a sense that much of the increased communication delivers little extra in the way of quality. The remark made some thirty years ago in a British Library funded research project is even more apt today: *There is too much publication of trivia based on inadequate evidence published by university researchers, who need to publish to progress. Find some criteria other than publication, as so much is being published that it is getting in the way of communication* (INFROSS, 1971).

People, subject to time pressures and vast amounts of potentially relevant information indulge in what is best called information gambling or information skimming. This involves taking onboard just enough information to get by with, or resorting to the reading of information surrogates or bites, book blurbs and reviews, abstracts and summaries of documents. *There is a trade off between what you can do with and what you can cope with. You only know about missed information when the crunch comes.* Overload also engenders a sense of hopelessness amongst those people suffering from it. *Information just overwhelms people – it makes them aware that their ability to change anything is zero. What's the point of knowing about things if you can't change anything? Who needs all that information?*

The lesson for the information professional here is that most people are not short of information *per se* – they generally have a surfeit of it. Where they typically need help is not in retrieving even more of it, but in digesting and screening out what they get. To bury people further in the information mire is a fast track to losing your job.

6. Collecting the Data

Data collection methods have to be given long and hard consideration, because of the cost and quality implications. Methods determine results, and this is never truer than in the case of information needs assessments. The data gathering method determines the type and quality of the data collected, and to obtain an accurate and comprehensive picture of need, it is necessary to select methods with care and adopt as wide a range of methods as possible to provide the necessary triangulation and reach. Inevitably, too, the choice of methods is determined not just by the issue being studied (information needs), but also by the information community being investigated. Thus, there is little chance of getting busy and self-important practitioners, like journalists, politicians or lawyers to subject themselves to the kind of examination that information researchers subject students to – diaries, for instance. Also, academics are generally a captive audience (and, hence, a much loved group amongst researchers), whereas practitioners and the general public certainly are not – that has an impact on choice as well. Sometimes, however, there is little choice but to accept what is to hand, what is cheap. In recognition of this a wider range of methods that would normally be recommended will be discussed and evaluated.

Probably, the real key to successful information needs analyses lies in understanding the data capture methods involved and learning how to master them. That is why this section merits so much space. When it comes to information needs there are four methods that will yield the necessary high quality data: interviews, questionnaires, diaries and observation. But really the interview is the real star. It is very much a case of horses for courses. If need is the horse then the interview is the course. Interviews – particularly the in-depth, open-ended interview, offer a fuller, richer and, possibly, more trustworthy source of data than all the rest. In fact, most of the methods employed by the information profession concern the monitoring of information use and information-seeking behaviour: citation analyses, computer log analysis and library use statistics are the popular methods. Such methods are closer to hand, generally already set up (routine) and provide copious amounts of data – always an attractive managerial characteristic. These methods should be used cautiously – because of the large number of problems associated with their use, and, ideally, linked to more appropriate methods, like interviews, for they can alert us to only a few of the needs characteristics, and then only imperfectly. Use indicators can be helpful in framing or raising questions for the needs interview or questionnaire.

Interviews

No research method is entirely free from problems, but interviewing must surely have the fewest. Interviews can probe for both qualitative and quantitative data. Furthermore, interviews have a habit of throwing up the unexpected, things that were not asked about – but with hindsight needed. With a good interview, the interviewee helps shape the scope and nature of the proceedings. And, of course, there is no real substitute for the method when it comes to studying non-use for, by definition, there are no beguiling numbers or transactional logs to help here. We must not be guilty of assuming that users are in the majority or the most important people.

There are many types of interview – the very fashionable focus groups, telephone interviews, group interviews, and the recommended one – the face-to-face, open-ended in-depth interview.

The face-to-face, open-ended in-depth interview.

The specific attractions of this form of interview are:

- crucially, data comes in the words of the interviewee. Too often, as in the case of questionnaires, individuals are shoehorned into forms of words devised by the interviewer, and, consequently, an unwanted or unwarranted bias intrudes. Possibly no user would ever have expressed themselves that way. The researcher puts words in the mouths of users and then proceeds to describe what users said in the vocabulary they fed them with in the first place. That is just a little incestuous. And that way you get little that is truly memorable or interesting. What chance is there of getting the comment the author received when interviewing a senior partner of an accountancy firm about end-use: trying to

112

explain why he never searched online systems himself he said: *I know how to make coffee, but I don't.*

- the opportunities it provides to question, explain and reflect: thus enabling the comprehensive exploration of complex issues like information needs and information-seeking behaviour;

- that full and complete responses to questions are more easily obtained through prompting;

- the observational opportunities it provides when interviews take place in the workplace, as they should. You can double your information, treble your insight, the moment you step into someone's office or workspace. Non-verbal communication can also be taken into account – telling us for instance how strongly people believe in what they are saying;

- the in-depth interview is especially powerful when the territory is unfamiliar – and with needs this is the case, almost by definition.

- high response rates can be obtained and it is the only method for getting information from some people. There is a problem getting high-status people to fill in questionnaires. There can be much less of a problem obtaining their agreement to be interviewed, especially if it is over lunch or coffee. A student of the author's, interested in Soap operas discovered this for herself when she managed to obtain interviews with the editors of Neighbours, Coronation Street and Brookside. The real problem with interviewing is in pinning us-

ers down to a time to interview them – practitioners in particular can be very busy.

The open-ended in-depth interview in practice

Open-ended interviews are characterised by their
open, wide-ranging questions and their loose, flex-
ible and unstructured format. Topics are explored
in depth on a one-to-one basis, with the interviewer
very much taking a back seat. Interviewees are
given the space to air their views in comfort. The
ratio of interviewer to interviewee contribution
should be 10:90, but possibly 20:80 in the case of
reticent interviewees or non-users – where more
prompting might be needed. What is being sought
are attitudes, opinions, facts and examples – and
often in that order. The real gems to be quarried by
the method are forms of words, expressions and
quotes. They are the diamonds in this methodological mine. Despite the wide-ranging and unstructured nature of the interviews, it is still
important to be consistent in interview approach
between interviewers, and across different interviewees.

Needs interviews are typically of around 30-60 minutes long, but they can last an hour and a half if
the interviewee is particularly talkative, or is known
to the interviewer. On the other hand, where a
person's time or patience is limited, or where the
interview pertains to a single search query, they can
be completed in 15-20 minutes. By definition time
is an important part of the method's success so one
should always be wary of reducing the interview
length. For the reasons mentioned above, interviews

should be held in a person's office. Getting people to talk long and hard about information today is generally not difficult. It is so topical that everyone wants to talk about it. In fact, by judicious questioning it is possible to use, for instance, the Internet, to explore a whole range of information phenomena that were once thought to be out of bounds in discussions with end-users. The Internet has to be the information equivalent of the Trojan horse. The opportunities for a comprehensive investigation of the entire communication system are there and should be readily grasped.

The user need framework proposed should function as a template through which data can be fed and evaluated, and should only be loosely used as an interview (or questionnaire) schedule. The framework alerts you to the data you need and the relevance of the data that you are getting – it acts as a filter, a place to collect and classify data. It is possible to use the framework for direct questioning at the end of the interview when a bridge has been built, when an understanding of the job has been obtained and when some information leads have been obtained. During a well run interview, data are likely to be volunteered on most, if not all, of the needs topics.

An example to illustrate the point. This is what an interviewee said as a result of a question concerning information overload which followed on from them recounting all the information inputs that came into a newspaper. *The presence of such vast quantities of information can lead to problems other than trying to digest/process it. Indeed, it can lead also*

*to an unbalanced view on events. For the danger is to
rely on the incoming paper flood and in so doing obtaining a far too institutional viewpoint on events. Take
the example of* The Guardian's Education *correspondent. For a start he would get about a metre and a half
of post a day. Masses will be coming from educational
institutions, from pressure groups, trade unions. It is
all institutional, it's all about providing education —
little of it is consumer oriented. It is not about what is
going on in the classrooms, it's not about what parents
are wanting etc. To get that information you must leave
the office. But that takes a tremendous act of will, for
the pressure is to stay in the office and read the post
and take the phone calls.* Apart from the graphical
description provided, the answer also discloses an
unexpected connection between information overload and the viewpoint of information sources.

It is sometimes said that there are no real rules to
interviewing. This is not true; and the rules have to
be obeyed if the interview is not to become stilted,
boring, unproductive, uncomfortable etc. Because
the interviewer is going into the fray with a small
number of broad questions and relying on the dy-
namics of the interview process to reveal as much
as possible, it is absolutely essential to capture, from
the very beginning, the person's interest and to make
them relax. Small talk usually helps. Curiosity,
empathy and compliments are important as well.
There are other important things that can make
the interview a success:

1.   The interviewer should never convey the impression that they are promoting the commodity,
system or idea (information in our case) that they

are enquiring about. If they do – even unintention-
ally – they will be type-cast, and the interviewee
might well try to please, or, in the case of non-users, either lie or shut-up completely. What should
be done to overcome the problem is to start by questioning the interviewee about their job, their work
and the problems they are experiencing. Virtually
everything they say will have an information needs
and information-seeking connotation – you can
then take each comment and mentally run it
through your analytical framework and tick it off.
It is only through the interaction between interviewee and interviewer that high quality data
emerges – for statements concerning information
need are seldom on the tip of the tongue, or crafted
with well-chosen prose. Through people recounting experiences – of a typical day perhaps – profit-
able lines of communication open out, and
genuinely new and interesting data emerges. They
will mention sources of information and systems
as a natural part of the discussion – anecdotes,
cases, examples alert the interviewer to a characteristic of information-seeking behaviour. Any topics not covered can be swept up at the end, by which
time the person should be so immersed in talking
about their work or problem (and its information
requirements) that they lose their inhibitions, and
are sure enough of their ground not to be easily
led.

Where, because of shortage of time or the demean-
our of the interviewee, the normal preliminaries
have to be dispensed with and the points have to
be made very quickly, it is useful to pose a neutral,
balloon-type question, such as, "The authority/

validity of information has merited a lot of discussion recently; what is your opinion on this?" This has an obvious value of 'helping' those for whom information plays a small part in their information-seeking behaviour to declare as much, while still permitting enthusiasts to put their case with relish. Another quick approach is to place before the user an item of relevance in the news, for example copyright, dumbing down, and build a line of questioning around it. This requires some preparation, and newspapers provide an excellent source of questions.

Once users find out the questions are about them and not you (or 'your' systems) they generally enjoy the experience. They find the questioning – and the periods of reflection that go with it – intriguing and stimulating and often come out of the interview feeling that they have been involved in an (information) counselling session. How did I do? is a typical response. Wanting to talk about the interview afterwards is another common reaction. Indeed, when the pressure of being recorded and being 'formally' interviewed comes to an end, many interviewees open up and talk at length, generally about the wider issues – the way information technology is changing their workplace, for instance. Of course, all this should be recorded.

2.   Probing is an essential part of an open-ended interview. Its function is to: (1) encourage further communication, (2) show interest, (3) make a direct bid for more information. What is required from the interviewer is motivation and direction, but without giving any signs that some responses

are more acceptable than others (otherwise you are back to the pitfalls of questionnaires). Probing questions follow up an interviewee's responses; they are particularly important in getting to the depth and detail of information required, but must be asked sensitively to avoid discomforting the interviewee. Postural signs of interest and acceptance – like nodding of the head – have a big role to play, especially in noisy workplaces. Brief assertions of understanding and interest: assenting comments like, 'I see', 'um-hm' play a part, in that they show that the answer is on the right lines, but has not been answered fully. You can go further and be rather more directional, though still retaining a neutrality: "in what way were your needs not met" – [clarification probe]. Silence can also be an effective – although sometimes disconcerting – probe, encouraging the interviewee to contribute more. Mirroring the thoughts of the interviewee can be very useful too – through this process they can see what they said more clearly and can make modifications if their words were interpreted wrongly or if they were hurried into saying the wrong thing.

One should not come away with the impression that open-ended interviews are problem-free and, indeed, some problems have already been alluded to. The real problem associated with the method is that it requires the researcher to step into a world outside their control, persuade and seek co-operation, ask (often personal) questions for which there are no stereotypical responses, and probe for data in unfamiliar territory. There are no prescribed or familiar lines of questioning – certainly not the sort that lend themselves to the satisfied v. satisfied formula so beloved of quantitative researchers. Open-ended interviews can be particularly challenging and unsettling for the novice interviewer. The challenge is to sustain a long conversation around a very general opening line and to keep the momentum going with the use of gentle prompts. By contrast, a structured interview with a long list of quite specific questions, provides a high degree of security and confidence (a methodological comfort blanket). It is dynamism and interactivity that binds the open-ended interview together.

There are other difficulties. Firstly, as with all interviews, the presence of the researcher of necessity affects what is said and done. This can lead to an artificiality in the proceedings. Secondly, establishing the necessary degree of informality in the interviewing process is easier said than done. The recording apparatus (see below), whether visible or not, may mitigate against this, as does the fact that interviewees will usually be aware of the general theme of the interview. Another factor precluding, to an extent, a degree of informality, is a presumed shortage of time on the part of the interviewee. In part, a recognition of this fact by the interviewer sometimes leads to an involuntary adoption of a more formal question and answer type formal interview, in an attempt to avoid interviewees thinking the exercise is a mere "chat" and, as such, something of a time waster. Unwanted formality can creep in despite the interviewer's best efforts. Thus subjects sometimes naturally adopt the role of one required simply to respond to set questions, even when it is stressed that they are free to offer any observations and talk in general terms about their work, and that there was no schedule of questions. Apart from stating at the outset that the exercise is not to be regarded as an "interview" as such, other tactics can be adopted to make the subjects feel more at ease and able to talk a little more naturally.

Thirdly, there is the problem of incomplete replies. As with any interview, participants are understandably unable always to give complete accounts of their information need. It is noticeable how many interviewees apologise for not remembering more, as these quotes illustrate: "I use the Internet much more than I've described ... I can't remember any examples ... I'm afraid I've got a poor short term memory". Returning to each interviewee a full transcript of their interview can provide much help with obtaining more complete and richer data from subjects.

Finally – and related to three above, privacy and confidentiality problems can arise. Thus discussing e-mail (to whom? how often? why?) may appear intrusive, as it would with "conventional" mail. Similarly, groups like journalists, analysts or politicians, are not noted for their openness concerning the material they are currently working with, and sometimes do not like discussing what they are doing.

Recording

Open-ended interviews raise the problem of how to capture the data: essentially, whether to use notebook or tape recorder (or both)? The use of a tape recorder brings with it the problem of making the interviewee feel uncomfortable, perhaps stifling some of the more sensitive responses. And it can prove a distraction (especially when the tape needs changing). Interviews are intrusive anyway; taping them may make them seem doubly so. One person interviewed was so wary of being taped he taped the interview too. Some people – especially non-users – might not respond at all if they know that every word they utter is being captured for further use. Non-users might feel that they have somehow failed – and do not want to 'broadcast' that fact. In addition, transcription times can be horrendous (allow 4-6 hours for each one hour interview) – something of real concern when several hundred interviews are being conducted. However, if the real data diamonds – the quotes, are to be captured then some taping is necessary. Also, if an interview session is being taped, then the interviewee is freer to think about the next question or interact with the interviewee. This is of particular benefit to novice researchers. With rapid developments in voice recognition software and digital tape recorders, maybe, some of these problems will simply fade away.

The big advantage of a notebook, as opposed to tape, is that it is not so unobtrusive, you can take it out quickly (for the impromptu interview), you are much closer to your data and you are editing as you go along, so less typing is involved later. People are also generally impressed by the fact that you are taking notes, that something they said was so important as to warrant the interviewer taking it down. Notes should even be taken during taped interviews, both as a back-up in case of poor quality recording and to add a degree of authority to the respondents' answers. To minimise the problems associated with tape recording the interviews, it is recommended that a pocket memo tape recorder, with a lapel mike, which could also be detached and placed on a holder on a table, should be used. This means recording is rather more discreet. The tapes the pocket memo uses are of a type that could be used in a professional audio-transcription system. Verbatim interviews can be transcribed directly into a word-processing package by an experienced typist.

Other forms of interview

There are other types of interview. There is the street/shopping mall interview so liked by polling organisations and market research companies. They are really nothing more than a spoken questionnaire which guarantees a certain level of response and representation. The interviewee selects from a range of options; opinions and attitudes outside the strict parameters of the study are not solicited or welcome. Within the profession such interviews are used largely by public libraries, who may find it difficult to interview people in their offices or homes or get them to fill in questionnaires on the premises.

Group interviews (including focus groups)

Group interviews deserve consideration, and one specialist type of group interview – the focus group, is certainly getting that. They have much to offer and are especially useful when time and funds are restricted. Group interviews are characterised by their free range and high levels of interaction. The interviews tend to have legs and can run on irrespective of the intervention of the interviewer. The role of the interviewer is diminished and less instrumental in the proceedings, so reducing the opportunities for spoon-feeding and bias. The interviewer can sit back, observe and note the interaction between interviewees. In many respects the interviewer takes on the role of referee. Interviewees like group interviews because they feel less threatened, bolstered as they are by their friends and colleagues. Users, who because of the age or seniority of the interviewer, might feel intimidated on a one-to-one basis soon loose their inhibitions in a group. Children are a case in point. They are less likely to subscribe to the perceived expectations of the interviewer. Group interviewing also provides for what sociologists call triangulation: it is clear by looking at the rest of the group whether the others accept a view that is being expounded. A lot of help can be expected in the clarification of the issues being considered: participants re-phrase and explain questions on behalf of other members of the group who might not have understood the crux or objective of the question.

There are two main problems associated with group interviews:

(1) scheduling things so that you can get half a dozen or more busy people together;

(2) recording the process – transcribing a tape on which many people are speaking, sometimes all at once – is not easy and takes a long time.

Focus groups are a form of group interview and em-
body many of the characteristics and virtues of the
open-ended, face-to-face interview. They are very
fashionable, thanks to the media publicity that has
arisen as a result of their use by political parties,
especially the Labour party, in taking the political
pulse of the voting public. Focus groups are discussions set up to explore a specific range of issues,
such as consumer's views and experiences with
regard to a particular hot topic – the Internet, for
instance. They may be made up of people from a
pre-existing group (students, for instance) or they
could be complete strangers. In the context of information need studies it would probably be ad-
vantageous to recruit participants who knew each
other – that way they could relate more easily.

Focus groups differ from the generic group interviews in that they have a moderator or facilitator
rather than an interviewer and that the data generated is said to be richer and more authentic. The
role of the moderator is to keep things flowing,
encourage interaction and ensure that things
emerge spontaneously. The question and answer
format is jettisoned and the participants replace the
interviewer as the dynamic. Data obtained from
focus groups are particularly rich because of the
context within which they are generated – resulting directly out of the minds and interactions of
the participants. Researchers are agreed that focus
groups generate spontaneous responses.

The key to success, of course, is to ensure that
everybody participates, feels relaxed and a momentum is established. Ice-breaking autobiographical

introductions and giving participants material that would stimulate discussion – quotes for instance, may be resorted to. The timing of moderator interventions is plainly important too. Focus groups also have a role in establishing frames of reference and assist in question framing for interview schedules and questionnaires.

Telephone interviews have become popular in recent years. As people feel more and more comfortable about conducting business over the phone then interviewing them over the phone becomes an increasingly attractive option. You get all the spontaneity that you get from face-to-face interviews, but you can do more interviews because you do not have to travel. Such interviews do not sit well with everyone because there is still a sense of double-glazing selling about them. But you would probably not cold-call someone for an information needs interview. Agreement and a time to phone would be obtained in advance. Phone calls should be limited to half an hour and should be taped – talking on the phone and taking notes at the same time is not easy. The advice of telesales people is that to succeed at this form of interviewing you need to be assertive and give the interviewee a sense of the importance of the exercise.

Questionnaires

Inevitably, if large numbers of geographically scattered people are being surveyed, time and resources dictate that questionnaires should be used. But in some respects they are unsuitable for the task in hand, and interviews are probably still required to pilot the questionnaires.

The other main reasons for using the method are:

- they provide quantitative and outwardly impressive data – numerous tables, graphs and figures can be generated;
- personal factors are largely removed from the questioning process;
- people are given time to consider the questions and to collect the necessary data;
- they are a boon for the shy and timid;
- much of the work appears to be done for you by a large number of people, many of whom might be quite important.

The chief problem associated with the method is that it is extremely difficult to produce a good questionnaire. Specifically:

- it is very difficult to formulate questions that are completely free from jargon (when asking about use of information systems or sources, for instance);
- bias and leading questions all too easily creep into question framing;
- it is very difficult to be certain that people understand the line of questioning and ambiguity frequently occurs. In an attempt to simplify, questions can become lightweight – sometimes not really worth asking. In particular attempts to obtain use/needs data can descend into vague categorisation – e.g. satisfactory, very satisfactory;

- response rates can be notoriously low, especially where busy practitioners are concerned (bulging in-trays tend to compete for attention and have a habit of burying questionnaires). You would be lucky these days to get a response rate of more than 40%. Stamped addressed envelopes, brevity, prizes (book tokens, for instance), offers of a copy of the survey findings, chasers, good timing and an offer of anonymity can improve response rates. However, the best response rates come from a well-designed questionnaire, that engenders interest on the part of the respondent and goes to a group that has not been targeted before, or who may feel that they will benefit directly from the exercise

Probably the most extensive questionnaire study on the topic of information needs was conducted as part of the Investigation of the Information Requirements of Social sciences (INFROSS) research project. During this project over a thousand individuals filled out questionnaires of nearly a hundred pages in length. This level of co-operation is highly unusual and is largely explained by the fact that the target group – social science academics, were experiencing big problems in coming to terms with an information explosion that resulted from the expansion in higher education that occurred at the time, and felt that their answers might lead to an improvement in their condition. The fact that they were largely an uncanvassed group helped too.

The Internet and its ability to reach out to a huge population with ease – and with little cost, has given the questionnaire survey a considerable boost. There are E-mail delivered questionnaires and those associated with the use of a Web site.

Observation

Observation is a particularly suitable method for gathering basic information about how, when and why information is used in organisations. The need to witness the whole information process in the round and to see the live interaction between an individual and information system means one thing: that users have to be observed in a work setting. Observation is ideally suited to studying: (a) communication in the office environment; (b) situations in which a lot of information is transmitted and received orally. Other attractions are:

- The people being surveyed do not have to do anything, other than give their permission to be observed – not always forthcoming, of course.

- Observation can prepare the ground for interview or questionnaire study. In these circumstances observation provides the investigator/question framer with an understanding of the circumstances surrounding the objects being studied. It also helps to establish the credibility of the investigator.

- You obtain a direct and unfiltered/unedited view (watching a play rather than asking the actor what happened).

- There is not the impediment of formalised language. People are not being asked questions.

Wilson and Streatfield (1980) pioneered the method to good effect with social workers. Since then it has been very much neglected. There are of course problems with the method.

- The very act of observation changes the nature of what is being observed. It may interfere with normal behaviour and provide a false, 'on my best behaviour' picture. Anyone who has been visited by the numerous panels of inspectors that inhabit all levels of education these days will know that it does change things. Lectures start on time and lecturers turn up in suits. Proponents of the method argue that while there is an initial period of unreality, this soon goes as the subject gets used to the shadow.

- Observation does not work very effectively if staff are largely desk-bound, inactive or if they spend long times at a single activity, like writing. It works best in busy environments, where the observer is easily forgotten. It works well in the open-plan newsrooms of newspapers, for example.

- Observation will not be very effective if the status of the observer imposes a threat to the subjects being observed. Imagine being observed by your boss – there is an implicit judgement being taken about your performance. More than one observer and the feeling of threat increases considerably.

- There is the problem of accurately describing and interpreting an event – how you interpret actions.

- So much is likely to happen while an observation is taking place that there is a need to focus only on the things that pertain directly to the observation brief. This cannot be easy when studying communication, because much of what happens could be of value – and sometimes you will not know until later.

- Observation is extremely time-consuming, frequently it is undertaken on a small-scale basis. You cannot really observe on a large scale, therefore it is difficult to generalise the data. Of course, you might spend a day observing and see very little.

- It can be difficult to filter information and focus – in these cases a rigid schedule is a must.

- Problems occur in interpreting behaviour. Take intent as an example: a group member is asking a question concerning the implications of a proposed solution to a problem. An observer ignoring intent might classify this as information-seeking, but one who takes intent into consideration might code it as attacking the solution.

Diaries

Diaries in a methodological sense are simply self-recorded observations and they are generally used as a substitute for questionnaires and interviews.

Diaries are not used a lot in our field, but are very popular in mass communication studies. This is partly because of the high degree of co-operation required and partly because researchers shun what they regard as being a low-tech method. But they do have a role to play, especially in understanding the information-seeking behaviour of children and students. Typically studies have employed diaries to monitor library use – activities performed, areas visited and satisfaction levels; time spent reading or browsing; actions taken after a book or reference had been found in a library.

In information science the diaries used have typically been highly structured.

The attractions of diaries are:

- They provide very specific data and very close to the point of action – actions and reactions to events can be recorded at the time of occurrence.

- They are good at getting at people's intentions and then comparing them with the information outcomes.

- You can collect a lot of data over a relatively short period of time.

The main problems associated with their use are:

- There is the issue of authenticity and bias – the editing of events by the diarists at a conscious and unconscious level.

- There is a question mark over their accuracy and completeness. How diligent will people be in maintaining them? – we know that busy people are the worst at filling them in.

- Obtaining a representative sample can be a problem. Volunteers tend to be a small self-selecting group.

- Maintaining motivation and interest over time is difficult. There can be a big drop-out rate, leading to an even more self-selecting group. One solution is to use a large sample over a relatively short time period. Another solution is to pay people for their co-operation (on completion, of course).

- Unless a structured diary form is used analysis of the data can be difficult and time-consuming.

Transaction log analysis

Transaction log analysis is the automatic monitoring activity of the computer system. Transaction logs tell us how users interact with computer systems. Logs only chart information-seeking behaviour at the terminal. From these logs it is possible, though sometimes dangerous, to ascribe particular forms of information-seeking to the user – and then go a step further and make statements about their information need. Needs characteristics, such as: the requirement for very current information and speed of delivery, the size of the information appetite, and whether highly processed information is wanted can sometimes be read into the logs. Constraints on information-seeking, like lack of time to search and digest the information may also be inferred. Despite the fact that transaction log analysis has been with us since the late Sixties – introduced to study systems' performance – it is only really since the Eighties, when the widespread introduction of OPACs and CD-ROMS into educational institutions gave researchers lots of motives and opportunities to study end-user searching, that it has become really popular.

Attractions of logs

- Not a lot of labour is involved. Having said this, though, while the actual collection of the data is sometimes simplicity itself – tempting the researcher to bite off more than they can chew, the subsequent analysis can be long, painstaking and frustrating.

- To a profession generally starved of hard statistical data, the sheer volume and level of detail that can be captured is beguiling. Surveys can never hope to match logs in this. To be able to describe searching characteristics in terms of hundreds or thousands of incidences, rather than dozens of them, gives log studies a certain weight and authority – not always warranted, of course.

- The objectivity of the method is one of its strong points: users' attitudes towards librarians and the system do not affect the result.

- The method is unobtrusive: no one is likely to refuse to take part in the study – largely because they do not know that it is going on, so there are no problems of low responses or biased samples. However, there are some big ethical questions to consider: do you inform all users as to what is happening, then what happens if some refuse to co-operate? Logs shaved of individual identifiers, have much less value.

- Logs tell it as it was, not, as is the case with interviews and questionnaires, as what was remembered.

- Logs enable direct and detailed head-to-head comparisons of the searching behaviour of user groups – men/women, intermediaries/ end-users.

Problems with logs

- The superficial nature of the data. Yes, big numbers are there, but what it all means is not always clear. Logs simply plot a particular form of behaviour, and even then, it is not always possible to point to a motive or reason for a particular search operation. Logs do not record users' needs or intentions, nor do they measure their satisfaction: to establish these things we must interview or send out questionnaires.

- It is difficult to assign data to an individual user or even a category of user, especially in the case of on-line open-access stations, where logging on and off is rarely undertaken.

- When interpreting the raw data, there is always the danger of reading too much into logs. Take the duration of a search session. What does it actually tell you? Does a slow search mean a poor search or a thorough search? Does a fast search mean an efficient search or a skimpy search?

Log metrics

- *Measures of use.* Obviously one of the major points of interest in all user evaluations is whether systems are being used. However, use can be measured in a variety of ways. The following indicators are commonly used: (a) search sessions conducted; (b) individual searches conducted; (c) on-line transactions made during a result of a search; (d) connect time.

- *Measures of satisfaction.* This is probably the most controversial log measure. Computer logs give no direct evidence of how successful searches were or how satisfied users were with their searches, but they do provide some clues. There is the number of records displayed. Something positive can be read into the fact that records were actually displayed as a result of a search. However, this does not merit as a strong measure of satisfaction, for allowances have to be made for the fact that negative searches can be positive, and that a display of records does not necessarily mean that useful records were found. Use itself is, of course, some measure of satisfaction.

- *Measures of expertise.* This points largely to constraints in meeting information needs. Expertise or skill can be demonstrated in a variety of ways. The traditional way of determining this has been to examine the range of commands being utilised. The underlying assumption being that the more commands used the more expert the searcher. This is easily determined, as too is the number of input errors made (when entering commands and terms) – another possible indicator. The other possible signs are not so easily assessed, they are: the appropriateness of the commands used; the structure of the search query (number and quality of terms, construction of statement); and the appropriateness of file selection and willingness to change files. However, on-line expertise and satisfaction with the product of a search does not necessarily go hand-in-hand. End-users or 'players' with minimal skills still achieve high rates of satisfaction.

- *File selection.* Single, blinkered and inappropriate source selection is often thought to be a hallmark of end-user searching. Equally, the judicious use of files and file switching is held to be the hallmark of the expert searcher. From logs, it is easy to spot file changes and monitor the number of files selected, but it is not so easy to determine whether the files selected were appropriate

- *Time of searching.* Logs provide a good deal of detail in this regard, enabling time, day, and month of searching to be determined. Time features strongly in many log analyses. We have already mentioned it as a means by which use and searching efficiency can be measured, and it can tell us something about the pattern and spread of searching. Of special interest here is the assertion that end-users leave searching to the last minute.

- *Subjects sought.* Through word frequency counts it is possible to gauge the subject characteristics of need. Though this should be treated with caution as people may use databases for quite specific purposes. Thus bibliographic databases are plainly used a lot for fact finding.

- *Currency.* By examining the dates of publication retrieved or how far back searches are conducted it is possible to obtain an idea of the age of material that is acceptable.

Web log analysis

With the rapid expansion of the Web researchers have moved away from OPAC evaluation to Web evaluation. While much of what has been said above also applies to Web logs, there are some special characteristics that need to be considered.

Web logging is made relatively easy by the fact that there is a large range of relatively cheap software that will do it for you – Analog and WebTrends are just two such products. Also, most servers will automatically generate Web site statistics based on the logs, but these are rather crude. With the distribution of free information being the Web watchword, use data replaces online revenues as the main metric. Log files are used to measure consumption, success and satisfaction amongst users or players. The measures of consumption are then fed into calculations for comparing Web sites, setting of charges to sponsors and the setting of web advertising rates. Web logs – still in their infancy, hold the key to personalisation developments on the Web and mobile phone.

What are Web log files?

Server computers record activity on clients that have logged on and mechanically record client requests for stored Web page(s). Client (computer) activity information is recorded automatically and routinely. The record of this activity is stored as a text file called a log file. The following line is a typical unresolved line from a log file and represents a single request by the client on the server.

Host	Date Stamp	Request Field	Status Field	Transfer Volume
193.150.189.1	[28/Apr/ 1999:11:06:48 +0100]	"GET / course/ msc/ ist/ 3.html HTTP/ 1.0"	200	7303

193.150.189.1 is the Internet Protocol (IP) number. This identifies the client computer and is recorded in the Host field. The number can be translated into a name using DNS lookup. DNS is the Domain Name Services and is a database of IP numbers and Domain names. A resolved name looks like: hadrian.guardian.co.uk. "Hadrian" is the name of a computer, "Guardian" – name of domain name organisation; "co" is the organisation type and "UK" the country code.

The host field identifies the user and is used to derive count statistics on the number of users and use. This field, for instance, provides user and use profile pie charts by location and profile pie charts by type of organisation. Further analysis of the client's host name will identify their exact name and address and hence allow direct contact with heavy users of an Internet site. *The Date Stamp* consists of three fields – date, time and offset from Greenwich Mean Time. From these fields it is possible to identify approximately how long the user has taken to read a page and how long the user has remained logged on to the site. Furthermore, looking at aggregates – counting the total amount of use per hour – a time distribution graph of users logged on can be drawn over hours, days and months. *The http request field* identifies the request type. "Get" for a normal HTML page and "Post" for forms and programs. Field also identifies the page or URL viewed by the user. This field is used to identify the most and the least popular pages viewed. Given a series of pages sorted by time, an idea of how the user has jumped from one URL to another can be derived and, hence, how the user has moved and searched through the site.

The status code field. This code is written to the log by the server to record the success or failure of the transaction. The frequency of status code is graphed and can inform the site administrator of the number of error codes. *Transfer Volume:* this field gives the number of bytes downloaded to the client's computer.

Never has use data been so important to so many, yet never has use data been so problematical. These are some of the problems:

1. The data are anonymous and aggregated. What the logs record are computers interacting with computers, not an individual interacting with a computer. Instead of a user ID and password you have an IP address. While it is relatively easy to translate this number into a domain name all you can really discern is the location of the computer, the name and type of organisation to which it belongs. Plainly a single person or a group of people may use this computer. Furthermore, there is increasing use of allocating computers in an organisation with a floating IP address. With floating IP addresses an IP address is allocated to a computer as required and will be allocated to another computer when it becomes available. If a computer is allocated a floating IP address the IP number cannot be assumed to be associated with a particular computer hence it is difficult to determine whether an IP address represents a single computer or many computers. Floating IP addresses make it particularly difficult to monitor/track a user over time and renders calculations based on repeat use inherently unstable. Location too is problematical because an IP registration address need not have any bearing on the computer's actual

location. A UK-based company may decide to register their IP address in the United States. It is estimated that 33% of UK users have a US IP address. Even when sites have a subscriber database it is rarely possible to relate this information to the logs. The database information itself, while useful, suffers from the fact that people provide false names (Tony Blair and Micky Mouse are regular users of The Times Web site it would seem) and subscribers are not necessarily users.

2. There are difficulties in determining whether use was intended and what actually constitutes use. Due to the imprecision of searching on the Web, the culture of surfing rather than searching, the numerous opportunities for linking and the hierarchical nature of much navigation, many sites and pages are 'used' but not in fact needed or relevant. Also a number of indicators present themselves: 'hits' – a line in a log file which represents a request by the client for a file on the server, page impressions or pages downloaded, visitors and time spent online. A "hit" is the crudest and perhaps the most misleading measure of them all. A single page viewed on the client's machine can generate several transaction hits on the server. This occurs because each image is downloaded as a separate request to the text. A single page viewed may generate up to 50 hits in the log file. Just counting the number of hits in the log files gives a misleading picture of use – it is a measure of consumption dependent on the number

of images on the site. A more effective measure of site use is to count the pages actually viewed by users – this is sometimes referred to as the page impression count. To estimate the number of page impressions all lines related to images need to be deleted from the log file. It is estimated that 65 to 75% of lines or hits in a log file will relate to images. Visitors are simply someone arriving at the site. The trouble is nobody signs off on the Web so we have to assume that, after a period of inactivity (normally thought to be 30 minutes), they have left. And, as we have mentioned already, all they leave anyway is a rather anonymous calling card (their IP address).

3. Caching. The client's machine will save a copy of pages recently viewed. When the client requests a page the client's browser will first check its cache for the page. Note the client would have to view the page at least once for that page to be in the machine's cache. However if the client computer uses its cache copy of the page then this will not be recorded by the server, as no requests would have been sent by the client machine. Hence a true picture of how the user negotiates the site cannot be made. The server only records hits of new pages viewed. It is estimated that up to 45% of pages viewed by the client are cached pages. Then there is commercial caching. Caching can be extended so that the pages viewed by one user can be made available to users on another machine. Here the cache is machine independent. Most

large commercial sites such as America On-line, Prodigy, and Compuserve use client in-dependent caching. And once a user requests a page, it is stored in memory at the request-ing site in case someone else wants to look at it. Again, this means use is underestimated.

4. That takes us nicely to the question of what constitutes a user on the Web. A user can be a spider or robot – and they are typically a site's biggest users. They can be identified, but how do you evaluate this kind of use and how do you compare it to the use of an individual, for example? You never had that problem with OPACs.

What is attractive about logs is the sheer volume of data generated, though this can prove a problem when storing and analysing the data; the fact that the data are collected routinely and without a great deal of effort; and their simplicity. What the logs are good at is highlighting patterns of use, identi-fying broad sweeps of information-seeking behav-iour that can be further investigated for their validity and significance during interview or ques-tionnaire surveys. They are also excellent at identi-fying change – something traditional research methods have never been very good at.

The most valuable analyses generated by Web logs:

- subject of pages downloaded
- most requested pages
- average page requests per day and hour
- average page requests per weekday

- most active day of the week
- average page requests per visit
- average duration of a visit
- visits by various types of organisations
- visits by country
- number of repeat visits
- number of unique visitors
- distribution by heavy, medium and light users
- pathways taken by players in negotiating the site.

Citation analyses

In many ways citations are rather like computer logs in that they provide stark and bald evidence of information use. Like logs the great attraction of citations is that they are available in large quantities. Interestingly, while citations are used as a surrogate for use data (especially in the case of journal use, which is much more difficult for a library to monitor than book use), they actually represent a qualified form of use. Generally, someone who cites a work not only has read it (used it) but, no doubt, selected it from a group of other works – so there is a quality and relevance judgement operating here also. Of course, documents may be consulted but not cited because they are rejected on grounds of value or direct worth. And, plainly, it is not simply the poor that are rejected, because some might be used but not cited – they go into the general consciousness and are not attributed to a specific idea, statement or quote. Plainly more items are used than cited. Although there are cases were items are not used, but are cited – students might refer to items in the lecturer's reading list to show that they have read the items or an author might refer to their own publications – self-citation, to boost their own intellectual standing.

Attractions of citations

1. A vast pool of inexpensive data are available that covers all subjects and all countries.

2. Much of the data collection is done for you – and what is more by the users themselves. Author-users leave behind a bibliographic fingerprint.

3. There is the added value that citations are also indicators of value and worth.

4. The data is relatively standardised and easy to analyse – the bibliographic record is a highly structured and regulated piece of use data.

5. You do not need any special equipment or permission – a big attraction in the case of students who increasingly have problems obtaining co-operation from outside bodies to conduct surveys.

Problems with citations

The chief problems flow from the fact that citations only provide a limited view of use for a relatively narrow band of specialist users. In strictly numeric terms there are probably more disadvantages than advantages associated with citation analysis, but in practice their widespread availability wins them many friends. The disadvantages are:

- Not all publications carry citations – those publications that do tend to be academic in nature. So practical/practitioner based fields, like social work, cannot fully profit from the methodology.

- Citations largely record the use of formal, external documents. Academic and scholarly practice largely dictates this. Personal sources, television and radio programmes are sometimes cited, but never in proportion to their use. There are some grounds for optimism though. Thus Web site citation seems to be becoming more popular – even newspaper correspondents, who have always fought shy of citing documents in their articles, seem happy to cite the Web (probably because it is fashionable).

- They are based purely on the activities of authors – the question that is begged is, do non-authors use the same sources?

- Citations only provide very limited details of use. Typically only author, subject, journal name, date, publication form, country, and language of publication can be discerned.

Major types of citation analyses

Obsolescence/decay

One of the prime and most direct uses of citation studies is to determine how far back in time authors search for their material. It is thought that relatively heavy use of the most recent literature is a hallmark of science and practitioner disciplines, where research, innovation and technology renders information obsolescent. There are problems associated with this interpretation, for the most recently published literature is subject to a much wider range of uses (current awareness and retrospective searching use), whereas the use of older items is much more restricted. There is also the problem of distinguishing between genuine decay and the appearance of decay given by a youthful rapidly growing subject field. This data has a lot of practical value, for librarians in helping them determine weeding, binding, remote storage policies. The 1970s' concept of the self-renewing library arose from a consideration of these data.

Subject analyses

Through these analyses we can determine: what subjects are being used; the scatter of subject use – the extent to which authors use a large/small number of subjects (the latter is thought to be a sign of a self-sufficient, well-defined field; the former a sign of interdisciplinarity); the extent to which authors are dependent on their own subject; and the subject fields most closely related to theirs. The data has a high practical value because it assists in library selection policies, helps determine the sweep of the literature search, and assists in classification and arrangement issues.

Form analyses

These analyses give us an insight into the preferred amount of processing and packaging. A high dependence on journals can alert you to a need for currency and speed of delivery, and this is thought to be a hallmark of a scientific discipline. Books citations signal the very opposite.

Country/language analyses

Country and language analyses can show how international the need is: whether information flows across frontiers (are we truly part of a global village?); the strengths of national relationships and how international a field is. International authorship and publishing can make it difficult to identify nationality.

Ranked lists

Ranked lists refer to journal titles. Here the interest largely lies in the scatter of citation over the journal population. Most analyses show a concentration of use on a relatively small number of journals: a minority of the literature accounts for the majority of use. This gives rise to the concept of a core literature. At one time this data was thought to be of enormous value for it enabled a librarian to cost their information provision on the basis of a library that would meet 75%, 90% or so of the demands (citations) made upon itself.

Library issue statistics

Not so long ago library issue statistics were the main weapon used in the drive to understand the user. Today, with computerised issue systems, this type of data is even easier to collect, but few information professionals subject this data to any form of serious analysis. The data is of course heavily flawed for it only concerns material that is borrowed in the library – and that largely excludes periodicals (though inter-library loan data can help here). Information consumed in the library, but not borrowed, is excluded and so logically, too, are office and personally obtained documents. At the end of the day, what you are evaluating is a small manifestation of information need.

7. Conclusion

The whole purpose of information needs assessments is to bring information customers to their rightful place at the forefront of the information chain; and, above all else, to ensure that information delivery is targeted, relevant and cost-effective. Far too much is going on in the information world for complacency to reign, yet we have been (and still are) complacent about our customers – real and potential. In the IT fog we seem to have lost our way and need to re-affirm our professional vows with our customers.

Use data, although very welcome, on its own cannot provide the big picture, the strategic data that is patently required. Nor will they tell us anything about the really big market – that of non-users. Use data has its rightful place – measuring the use of what is provided, but beware of employing use data as a substitute for needs data. Otherwise there is a danger of running into the blind alleys in which some information services find themselves. Thus, take public libraries: some argue that, because the elderly are the key user group in many public libraries, that there is little point introducing technology into the library because this group would not be receptive to it. Even if this was true, the plain fact is that the elderly forms such a significant user group because public libraries provide what they want - lots of hard-copy fiction. If you filled libraries with Internet terminals and CD stations then things would soon change, and you would find that the young would become the chief customers. So what value is obtaining only use data in a rapidly changing and expanding information environment?

The very personal nature of information needs assessments and the processes involved (the repeated interviewing, the questioning etc.) ensure that close contact is maintained between information service and information player. The reciprocal exchange of information will benefit both parties enormously - and will ensure that the information service is never isolated from the mainstream activities of the community it serves, for that is where the real threat to information services lies. The questioning process that underpins information needs assessments should be seen as a vital part of the modern information professional's armoury. In many respects what is being proposed is a form of information counselling - and it may well be that the information profession will find security and prosperity through it. Undoubtedly, people will do more of their own searching in future, but what they cannot do is to counsel themselves about their information needs - and that it is something that they will need in the dynamic, competitive and threatening information environment in which they will increasingly find themselves. Social counselling was very much the growth industry of the 1990s, and it is likely that information counselling will be the growth industry of the first decade of the new millennium.

For that to happen we have to move closer to our clients. At present no one is competing for this role, but this should not make us complacent. The methodology is there, the technology is there, the opportunity is there and sometimes the data are also.

Whether the interest and inter-personal skills are there is much less certain. However, feet-dragging on the part of information profession, will not slow the onward march of personalised information systems and services – and the information needs assessments that are such an essential part of them. It really is just a question of who does them. We shall know whether this has all come to pass when an evaluation of an information unit is conducted in terms of people satisfaction and not system performance, or when pride is shown in the quality and skills of the information players and not just the quality of the systems.

Information needs analysis has had a long history of neglect in the information profession, and much ground has been lost as a result. Even use studies – a poor relative, have not fared much better. This book has reviewed the factors that have led to this neglect and demonstrated why people (*I-players*) and their needs will soon emerge at the top of the information science and systems agenda. The irony is not lost that, if this should happen, it will be an information system – the Internet – and not information professionals, that will put it there. E-commerce should ensure it stays there. No matter, lost ground can still be made up. The Internet should put information needs there because: (a) it is only through an understanding of information needs and use, that the Internet's true potential can be unlocked; (b) it provides the mechanisms by which aspects of need and use can be routinely monitored.

If for any reason it is not the PC/Internet that raises the information needs stakes then it will surely be the digital mobile phone – those connected to computerised information services. The digital mobile phone offers a highly personal information service that is a much closer approximation to real life than PCs are. The mobile phone represents a genuinely popular (mass) platform for seeking and finding information. You cannot really say that of the PC, despite the giant strides it has taken towards this goal. What will surely drive the use of the phone as an information retrieval medium will be the vast and ever-increasing amounts of real-time information becoming available. That is why you need information on the move – infomobility. The logs from mobile phones will be particularly interesting for they offer a real prospect for mapping the individual's information-seeking behaviour.

A highly practical evaluatory framework and methodology has been proposed which will produce the necessary data. Used in conjunction with use data from the Internet, Intranets, mobile phones and digital television, at last, we can look forward to data of a quality and volume that we have long come to expect from information systems.

Finally, perhaps the profession's notorious neglect of the user can be explained in some way by the term itself. Such a general and vague term hardly reminds us of the primacy of the individual and the necessity to investigate the individual's information needs. The term *player* by contrast demands such an investigation. It sends all the right signals. And that is what this Web-based world is all about. Maybe, the solution lies with just changing one word. Now that sounds easy.

8. References and Selected Bibliography

Anon. Why don't the writers on *The Economist* have the guts to sign their articles. *The Times* 19th October 1984. p. 15

Bath University Library. *The Information needs of social workers. Investigation into information requirements of the social sciences. Research Report 4.* Bath: Bath University Library, 1971

Bath University Library. *Investigation of the information requirements of the social sciences. Report 1: Information Requirements of Researchers in the Social Sciences;* Vol 1 Text. Bath University, 1971.

Bawden, D. et al. Perspectives on information overload. *Aslib Proceedings* 51(8), September, 1999, pp. 249-255.

Belkin, N.J. and A. Vickery. *Interaction in information systems.* London: British Library, 1989 (chapter 2).

Beheshti, J. A longitudinal study of the use of library books by undergraduate students. *Information Processing & Management* 25(6), 1989, pp. 734-744

Brittain, J. *Information and its users.* Newcastle: Oriel Press, 1970.

Cronin, B. Assessing user needs. *Aslib Proceedings* 33(2), 1981, pp. 37-47.

Dervin, B. and Nilan, N. Information needs and uses. *Annual Review of Information, Science and Technology* 2, 1986, pp. 37-47.

Davis, D. New approaches to studying library use. *Drexel Library Quarterly* 7(1), January 1971, pp. 4-12

Dobrowolski, T et al. Mobile phones: the new information *medium*? *Aslib Proceedings* 52(6) June 2000 (forthcoming)

Ellis, D. Modelling the information seeking patterns of academics. *Library Quarterly* 63(4) Oct 1993, pp. 469-486

Glover, S. Media: Mystery of Mariella. *Evening Standard* 8th June 1994, p. 43.

Goodhall, D. Use of diaries in library and information research. *Library and Information Research News* 19(59), Spring 1994, pp. 17-21

Green, A. What to we mean by user needs? *British Journal of Academic Librarianship* 5(2), 1990, pp. 65-78.

Jackson, D. Anything you can recall, I can recall better. *The Independent* 26th January 1993, p. 14.

Julien, H. Constructing 'users' in library and information science. *Aslib Proceedings.* 51(6), June 1999, pp. 206-209.

Kay, W. Streetwise: Profile Geoffrey Mulcahy. *InterCity Magazine* June 1994, pp. 20-22.

Line, M.B. Designing libraries round human beings. *Aslib Proceedings* 50(8), September, 1998, pp. 221-229.

Line, M.B. Draft definitions: information and library needs, wants, demands and uses. *Aslib Proceedings* 26(2), 1974, p. 87

Line, M.B. Information requirements in the social sciences: some considerations. *Journal of Librarianship* 1(1) January 1969, pp. 1-19.

Line M. *et al. Information requirements of College of Education lecturers and schoolteachers*. (INFROSS Research Report 3). Bath; Bath University Library, 1971

McRae, H. They're going to set the lines buzzing. *The Independent* 4th November 1993, p. 20.

Marden, M and Nicholas, D. Information needs of parents. *Child Language and Teaching Therapy*, 13(3), 1997, pp.279-285.

Nicholas, D. *An assessment of stereotypical models of on-line searching behaviour: end-users. Case study practitioners: politicians and journalists*. PhD Dissertation. London: City University, 1995

Nicholas, D and Martin, H. Assessing information needs: case study of journalists. *Aslib Proceedings* 49(2) February 1997 pp. 43-52.

Nicholas, D, and Williams, P. The changing information environment: the impact of the Internet on information seeking in the media. In: *Information seeking in context, Proceedings on research in information needs, seeking and use in different contexts. 13th-15th August 1998, Sheffield*. Taylor Graham, 1999.

Nicholas, D, Huntington, P, Williams, P, Lievesley, N and Withey, R. Developing and testing methods to determine the use of web sites: case study newspapers. *Aslib Proceedings* 51(5) May 1999, pp. 144-154.

Nicholas, D. The information needs interview: a long way from library-use statistics. *Education for Information* 15(4), Dec 1997, pp. 343-350.

Nicholas, D. The Information Player in *Handbook of special librarianship and information work* edited by Alison Scammell. 8th edition. London: Aslib, 2000

Nicholas, D. Information systems vs information users. *Managing Information* 3(6), June 1996, pp.26, 31-33.

Nicholas, D and Rowlands, I., editors. *The Internet: its impact and evaluation. Proceedings of a forum held at Cumberland Lodge, Windsor Park, 16-18th July 1999.* Aslib, 2000.

Nicholas, D, Williams, P, Martin, H and Cole, P. *The media and the Internet.* Aslib, 1997

Nicholas, D. *et al. Online searching: its impact on information users.* London: Mansell, 1987. pp. 48-113

Nicholas, D and Huntington, P. Who uses Web newspapers, how much and for what? A log analysis of The Times/Sunday Times web sites. *NetMedia99 Conference: Proceedings.* London: City University, July 1999.

Renneker, M. A qualitative study of information seeking among members of an academic community: methodological issues and problems. *Library Quarterly* 63(4), Oct 1993, pp. 487-507.

Shinebourne, J. User needs, the new technology and traditional approaches to library services. *Journal of Information Science* 2(3/4) October, 1980, pp. 135-140.

Slater, M. *Information needs of social scientists.* London: British Library, 1989.

Stone, S. Humanities scholars: information needs and uses. *Journal of Documentation* 38(4), Dec 1982, pp. 292-313

Streatfield, D. Community workers and information: from national resources to neighbourhood advice. *Social science information studies.* 2(1) 1982, pp. 23-37.

Streatfield, D. Moving towards the information user: some research and its implications. *Social Science Information Studies* 3(4), 1983, pp. 223-240.

Streatfield, D. and Gee, V. Making information serve development: 2. Building bridges to information users. *Library Association Record*, 92(4), April l990, pp. 282-284.

Tannen, D. War of words. *The Guardian.* 27th April 1991

Truss, L. Too many words, too little said. *Interface. The Times* 7th April 1996, p. 3

Watts, S. Academics under threat from an electronic vision. *The Independent* 8th June 1994, p. 3.

Webb, S. Information strategy. *Information Management Report*. January 1994, pp. 9-11

Williams, R. Office slaves miss out on the office revolution. *The Independent* 4th July 1993, p. 5

Wilson, T and Allen, D. *Information seeking in context, Proceedings of on research in information needs, seeking and use in different contexts*. 13th-15th August 1998, Sheffield: Taylor Graham, 1999.

Wilson, T. On user studies and information needs. *Journal of Documentation* 37(1), 1981, pp. 3-15.

Wilson, T. and Streatfield, D. *You can observe a lot*. Sheffield: University of Sheffield, 1980.

Aslib Know How Guides